HEINEMANN HISTORY

BRITAIN AND THE GREAT WAR

STUDY UNITS

HEINEMANN
EDUCATIONAL

Rosemary Rees

Heinemann Educational Publishers,
Halley Court, Jordan Hill, Oxford OX2 8EJ
a division of Reed Educational & Professional Publishing Ltd

OXFORD PORTSMOUTH NH (USA) CHICAGO
MELBOURNE AUCKLAND IBADAN
GABORONE JOHANNESBURG BLANTYRE

© Rosemary Rees 1993
The moral right of the proprietor has been asserted

First published 1993

98 99 00 10 9 8 7 6

**British Library Cataloguing in Publication Data is available
from the British Library on request.**

ISBN 0 435 31284 7

Designed by Ron Kamen, Green Door Design Ltd, Basingstoke

Illustrated by Barry Atkinson and Jeff Edwards

Printed by the Bath Press

The front cover shows a First World War recruiting poster for
women ammunition workers.

Icon information

Every Unit in this book includes the following symbol. When a
section is filled in, it indicates the availability of extra
resources included in the accompanying *Assessment and
Resources Pack*.

For every Unit there is a Foundation Worksheet.

Acknowledgements

The author and publisher would like to thank the following for
permission to reproduce photographs:

Bildarchiv National: 2.2A
British Aerospace Airbus Ltd: 10.1A
British Legion: 1.1A
British Library: 9.2A
Camera Press Ltd: 3.3E, 5.1C
Hulton Deutsch Collection Ltd: 2.3B, 7.1A, 7.3A, 10.1F, 10.2F
Imperial War Museum: Cover and 3.1B, 3.2B, 3.3C, 3.4C and
D, 3.5A and D, 3.6A and D, 4.1A, B and C, 4.3A, 4.4A and D,
5.1A, 5.2A and C, 6.1A and F, 6.2 A and E, 6.3B and C, 6.4A,
C and E, 7.2A and E, 7.3C, 8.1A and D, 8.2B, C and D, 10.2A,
B, C and E
Leeds University Library: 4.2B, 9.2D
Rex Features: 1.1D
Sue Styles: 1.1B

The author and publisher would like to thank George Sassoon
for permission to reproduce 'The General', p. 14, 'The Dug
Out', p. 51 and 'Does it Matter?', p. 51, by Siegfried Sassoon;
Macmillan London Ltd for permission to reproduce 'Breakfast'
by Wilfrid Gibson on p. 50.

Thanks also to Dr John Pimlott, Senior Lecturer in the
Department of War Studies, Royal Military Academy
Sandhurst, for his invaluable comments on the original
manuscript.

*This book is dedicated with love to my late father, Ellis Dawson, who
first interested me in the past and what happened there.*

Every effort has been made to contact copyright holders of
material published in this book. Any omissions will be rectified
in subsequent printings if notice is given to the publisher.

Details of written sources
In some sources the wording or sentence structure has been
simplified to ensure that the source is accessible.
B. Bates, *The First World War*, Blackwell, 1984: 4.2C, 4.4B,
4.4E; Vera Brittain, *Testament of Youth*, Victor Gollancz, 1933:
6.1C, 9.2E; J. Brooman, *The Great War*, Longman, 1985: 4.2A;
W. S. Churchill, *The World Crisis 1911–14*, Thornton
Butterworth, 1933: 4.3B; Rev. A. Clark, *Echoes of the Great
War*, Oxford University Press, 1988: 3.1A, 7.1B, 7.2D, 7.3B,
7.3D; G. Coppard, *With a Machine Gun to Cambrai*, Imperial
War Museum, 1980: 3.3B, 3.5C; J. Ellis, *Eye Deep in Hell*,
Croom Helm, 1976: 3.5E, 3.6C; Michael Foss (Ed.), *Poetry of
the World Wars*, Michael O'Mara Books, 1990: 1.1C;
B. Gardner (Ed.), *Up the Line to Death*, Eyre Methuen, 1964:
3.2A, 4.4C, 5.2B; Wilfrid Gibson, *Collected Poems 1905–1925*,
Macmillan & Co London, 1926: p. 50 (lower right);
W. Griffith, *Up to Mametz*, Faber and Faber, 1931: 3.4A;
J. Hamer, *The Twentieth Century*, Macmillan, 1989: 2.3C;
Hansard, 1917: 10.1D; M. Holden, *War in the Trenches*,
Wayland, 1973: 9.1E; T. Howarth, *Joe Soap's Army Song Book*,
Longman, 1976: 6.1E; T. Howarth, *On the Western Front*,
Longman, 1976: 3.3A; R. Huggett, *Growing Up in the First
World War*, Batsford, 1985: 10.2D; D. Jones, *In Parenthesis*,
Faber and Faber, 1937: 9.2F; Nigel Kelly, *The First World War*,
Heinemann Educational, 1989: 2.2B, 9.1D; A. Kirkaldy,
Industry and Finance, Isaac Pitman, 1917: 10.1E; *Labour Leader*,
Independent Labour Party, 1917: 8.2E; A. Marwick, *Women at
War*, Fontana, 1977: 8.2A; A. Maurois, *Life of Sir Alexander
Fleming*, Penguin, 1963: 10.1B; A. S. Milward, *The Economic
Effects of Two World Wars on Britain*, Macmillan Educational,
1984: 6.3D; Sylvia Pankhurst (Ed.), *Workers Dreadnought*, East
London Federation of Suffragettes, 1918: 7.1C; Fiona
Reynoldson, *War in Britain*, Heinemann Educational, 1988:
6.1B, 6.1D; Joe Scott, *Medicine through Time*, Collins, 1970:
10.1C; Jon Silkin (Ed.), *First World War Poetry*, Allen Lane,
1979: 3.2A, 5.2B, p. 50 (middle), p. 51 (upper right); A. J. P.
Taylor (Ed.), *Lloyd George: a diary by Frances Stevenson*,
Hutchinson, 1971: 6.2C; G. Thomas, *Life on All Fronts*,
Cambridge University Press, 1989: 6.2B, 7.2B, 7.2C, 8.1B,
8.1C; *Wages and Conditions of Employment in Agriculture*, report
published 1919, 6.2D; D. Winter, *Death's Men: Soldiers of the
Great War*, Allen Lane, 1979: 3.5B, 3.6B, 5.1B; J. M Winter,
The Experience of World War One, Macmillan, 1988: 5.1D, 5.2D

CONTENTS

PART ONE   INTRODUCTION
1.1   Remembrance   4

PART TWO   WHY DID THE GREAT WAR BEGIN?
2.1   Alliances and Ambitions   6
2.2   Flashpoint Balkans!   8
2.3   War Plans and Mobilization   10

PART THREE   THE WESTERN FRONT
3.1   Stalemate   12
3.2   Trench Warfare   14
3.3   The Battle of the Somme, 1916   16
3.4   Life in the Trenches: Routine   18
3.5   Life in the Trenches: Clean and Healthy?   20
3.6   Life in the Trenches: Casualties   22

PART FOUR   THE WAR SPREADS
4.1   The British Empire   24
4.2   Allies and Enemies   26
4.3   The War at Sea   28
4.4   The War in the Air   30

PART FIVE   WEAPONS AND TACTICS
5.1   Artillery and Machine Guns   32
5.2   Gas and Tanks   34

PART SIX   THE GOVERNMENT
6.1   Recruitment and Conscription   36
6.2   Factories and Farms   38
6.3   Transport and Finance   40
6.4   Propaganda   42

PART SEVEN   THE PEOPLE
7.1   Food and Drink   44
7.2   Bombs, Spies and Invasion   46
7.3   Attitudes   48
7.4   War Poetry   50

PART EIGHT   WOMEN AT WAR
8.1   At the Front   52
8.2   Back Home   54

PART NINE   PEACE
9.1   The Final Offensive   56
9.2   Armistice Day: 11 November 1918   58

PART TEN   AFTERMATH
10.1   Gains   60
10.2   Losses   62

Index   64

1.1 Remembrance

Every November poppies are sold on the streets of Britain. They are sold, too, in pubs, offices, schools, factories, cafes, shops and garages. Do you know why?

The First World War ended at 11 o'clock on 11 November 1918. At that exact time on every 11 November in the years that followed, there was a two minute silence. Everything came to a complete standstill while people remembered the War and those who had been killed. Red poppies were sold to mark the day; the money was given to the Earl Haig Fund which helped war widows and the injured. Today, people remember those who died in both World Wars and all wars involving Britain since then on the Sunday nearest to 11 November: **Remembrance Sunday**.

In the years after 1918 war memorials were built in most villages, towns and cities. The names of all those who had been killed were carved on them for everyone to read. Where is your local war memorial?

A **SOURCE**

A modern-day poppy seller.

B **SOURCE**

The war memorial on the Scottish island of Raasay.

1914 – 1918
In Memoriam

In the years after 1918, towns and cities held local ceremonies of remembrance at their own war memorials. Men, women and children said prayers and sang hymns, laid wreaths of poppies, and watched parades of men who had fought. Services of remembrance were held in the local churches. Parades and services still take place on Remembrance Sunday.

A national war memorial, the Cenotaph, was built in London after the First World War. Here the same sorts of ceremonies are carried out on behalf of the whole country and the Commonwealth.

Everyone needs to remember the past. Sometimes it is our own private past we remember; sometimes it is the past of a nation. It is important that what we know about the past is accurate and true. We must know what happened, and we must know why it happened.

D

SOURCE

The Queen laying a wreath of poppies at the Cenotaph in London.

E

SOURCE

When I was a Girl Guide I was chosen to carry the Union flag at church parade one Remembrance Sunday. The whole Guide company followed me into church. I dipped the huge flag slowly in front of the altar when the boom sounded for the two minute silence.

Rosemary Rees remembers a Remembrance Sunday service when she was a girl.

C

SOURCE

In Flanders fields the poppies blow
Between the crosses, row on row
    That mark our place; and in the sky
    The larks, still bravely singing, fly
Scarce heard amid the guns below.

We are the Dead. Short days ago
We lived, felt dawn, saw sunset glow,
    Loved and were loved, and now we lie
    In Flanders fields.

The first two verses of a poem by John McCrae.
He was a soldier who died of his wounds in 1918.

Activities...

1 There are war memorials in most British towns and villages. What does this tell you about the First World War?

2 Look at Source B. In all, 36 men from Raasay fought in the war, and there is one line for each man killed. How many men came home, and what effect do you think this had on Raasay?

3 How does the poem, Source C, help to explain why poppies are used for remembrance?

2.1 Alliances and Ambitions

GERMANY

Germany's ruler, **Kaiser Wilhelm II**, wanted to make Germany a great power. He encouraged industry. By 1914 Germany produced more steel than Britain and almost as much coal. The Kaiser wanted Germany to have more land in Europe and an overseas empire. Most German people and politicians agreed with him. The German army was the strongest army in Europe. The Kaiser began to make the German navy powerful too. Some Germans thought that other European countries would begin to be afraid of the new, powerful Germany. They realised that Germany could come to be surrounded by enemies.

GREAT BRITAIN

In 1914 Great Britain seemed to be the richest and most powerful country on Earth. Industry prospered and trade flourished. The British Empire was the largest in the world. Countries in the Empire provided raw materials for Britain's industries and bought what Britain produced. The Royal Navy was the most powerful navy in the world. It kept the sea-routes between Britain and the Empire safe for merchant ships. It was ready to defend the Empire from attack. Most British politicians were worried by Germany's growing strength.

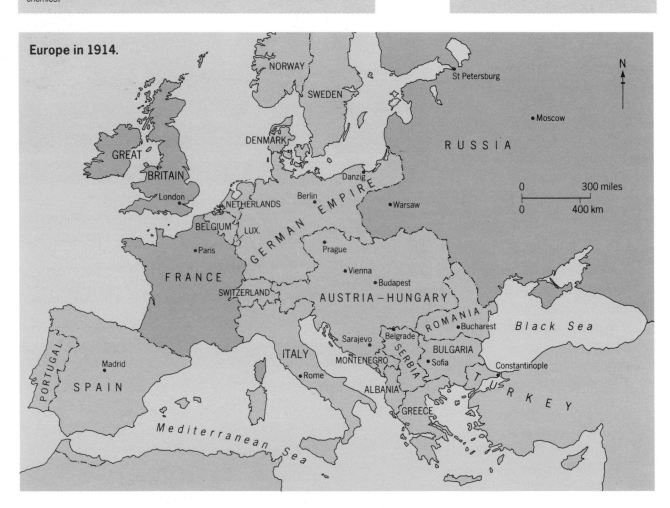

Europe in 1914.

FRANCE

The president, **Raymond Poincaré**, governed a country the size of Germany, with the second largest empire in the world. But by 1914 France could not match Germany's growing strength. French farms and factories produced less than German ones. Fewer babies were born. In 1870 France and Germany had fought a bitter war. France was defeated. The rich and fertile French provinces of Alsace and Lorraine became part of Germany. Many French people were desperate for revenge, but they were afraid of the growing strength of Germany.

AUSTRIA-HUNGARY

The emperor, **Franz Joseph**, ruled over 50 million people in a country with little heavy industry. His people were divided into at least 11 different nationalities, including Magyars, Czechs, Slovaks, Serbs, Croats and Slavs. Each had its own language and way of life. Many wanted to break free and form independent states. Franz Joseph was afraid that anything in Europe which encouraged nationalism would break up his empire.

RUSSIA

The Tsar, **Nicholas II**, ruled over the largest and one of the poorest countries in Europe. Russia was hard to govern. It was an empire of many different peoples, who all spoke different languages. Much of the land was not farmed because it was too cold. There was little industry. For a large part of the year the ports could not operate because the sea was frozen. So trade with the outside world was almost impossible. Russia desperately needed ice-free ports and modern technology.

HE WONT BE HAPPY TILL HE GETS IT

A

SOURCE

This British postcard shows the German Kaiser in his bath reaching for a piece of soap shaped to look like Europe. The postcard was printed in 1914.

The alliance system

Europe in 1914 was a dangerous place. The five Great Powers were divided into two strong and powerful alliances. They were about to fight each other in the most awful war the world has ever known. To understand how this happened, we must go back to 1879.

In 1879 Germany quarrelled with Russia. Germany was worried that Russia would attack, and so agreed with Austria that the two countries would help each other if either was attacked. Three years later, Italy joined them, and the **Triple Alliance** was formed.

This alliance upset France and Russia. In 1892 they agreed to help each other if either was attacked. Great Britain was worried about the situation in Europe and began to look for an ally. In 1904 Britain signed an agreement with France called the 'Entente Cordiale'. Three years later Britain made a similar agreement with Russia. The alliance between Britain, France and Russia was known as the **Triple Entente**.

By 1907 Europe was divided into two sets of alliances, the Triple Alliance and the Triple Entente. The countries in both alliances were well armed and powerful. It only needed one flashpoint for war to break out. This flashpoint happened, as you will see, in the Balkans.

Activities...

1 a Copy the grid below. Put the names of all five Great Powers in the left-hand column. Write down what each Power was afraid of, and what each Power wanted.

Great Powers	Fear	Ambition

b Was the alliance system made because of fear or ambition? Explain your answer.

2 a How would the Triple Alliance help Germany if Russia attacked?

b How would the Triple Entente help France if Germany attacked?

3 Look at Source A.
a What serious point was the artist trying to make?
b Was this the main reason why the alliance system was set up?

Flashpoint Balkans!

A SOURCE

Franz Ferdinand and his wife, sitting in the back of the car, begin the drive to Sarajevo town hall.

Murder at Sarajevo

28 June 1914 was a warm and sunny day. It was the **National Day** of the Serbian peoples; it was also the wedding anniversary of Franz Ferdinand, heir to the throne of Austria-Hungary. Archduke Franz Ferdinand and his wife the Duchess Sophie were paying an official visit to the town of **Sarajevo**, in the province of Bosnia. Lurking amongst the crowds who came to cheer were students intent on murder. Suddenly one of them threw a bomb at the royal car. The bomb exploded in the road, injuring several people. Franz Ferdinand was furious. How dare people spoil his wedding anniversary and his wife's treat by trying to kill them! When the royal car reached the town hall he shouted angrily at the mayor and decided to cancel the visit immediately. He wanted to visit the injured, and then go home. On the drive back to the station the chauffeur took the wrong turning and stopped the car to reverse. One of the rebel students, Gavrilo Princip, was walking past. He aimed his pistol and fired at the royal couple. By 11.30pm Archduke Franz Ferdinand and his wife Sophie were dead. Six weeks later Europe erupted into war.

B SOURCE

I fired twice at Ferdinand from a distance of four or five paces. I raised my hand to commit suicide, but some policemen and officers seized me and struck me. They took me away, covered with blood, to the police station. I am not a criminal, for I destroyed a bad man. I thought I was right.

From a statement made by Gavrilo Princip at his trial.

The Balkans had once been ruled by Turkey. Turkey became very weak in the nineteenth century. Slav people living in the Balkans gradually drove out their hated Turkish rulers. New Slav nations – Serbia, Rumania and Bulgaria – were set up.

Austria-Hungary was afraid that Slavs living in Bosnia and other Balkan States within the Austro-Hungarian Empire would break away and join Serbia. This would mean the collapse of the Empire. To prevent this, Austria-Hungary wanted to control the Balkans.

Russia desperately needed to use ports on the Mediterranean Sea. This would make trade easier. Russia also needed to be able to sail its war ships out of the Black Sea in times of trouble. Russia needed to control the Balkans.

Germany needed oil for her industries. The Kaiser wanted to build a railway between Berlin and Baghdad (now the capital of Iraq) where there were rich oil fields. This railway would have to pass through the Balkans. Germany needed the Balkans to be friendly.

Gavrilo Princip was a member of the **Black Hand** – a gang dedicated to uniting all Slav peoples in the Balkans. Austria believed the Black Hand was supported by the Serbian government. The time had come to teach Serbia a lesson.

Countdown to war 1914

29 June Austria asks for German help
6 July Germany agrees to stand by Austria
23 July Austria sends demands to Serbia
25 July Serbia agrees to all demands but one
28 July Austria declares war on Serbia. Serbia asks Russia for help
1 August Germany declares war on Russia. France mobilizes
2 August Germany asks Belgium to let German troops through into France. Belgium refuses
3 August Germany declares war on France
4 August Germany invades Belgium

In just eight days four of the five Great Powers had declared war on each other. What would Britain do?

Activities...

1 At the start, the quarrel was between Austria and Serbia. Why, then, did:
  a Germany declare war on Russia?
  b Germany declare war on France?

2 Was Gavrilo Princip to blame for the First World War?

The Balkans in 1914.
1913) shows date of independence.

2.3 War Plans and Mobilization

All the Great Powers had made plans in case war broke out in Europe. The British plan was to send a small, well-trained force, the **British Expeditionary Force**, across the Channel to defend Belgium and France. France's **Plan Seventeen** was to begin an all-out attack on Alsace and Lorraine. Austria planned to pour huge armies over its border with Russia. Russia aimed to send its armies over the same border into Austria.

Germany feared a war on two fronts: against France and Russia. They drew up the **Schlieffen Plan**. Germany would first knock France out by a lightning attack through Belgium. German troops could then turn to deal with Russia. It was essential that France was defeated quickly before the slower Russian army could mobilize.

Each war plan had been worked out carefully. Speed was of vital importance. Each army had to be taken to the battle-front. Along with the men went their guns and all the supplies they were likely to need. In every country most people were sure the war that was starting would be over in weeks, and certainly by Christmas.

Belgium was a neutral country. This meant it would not take sides in any war. In 1839 Britain, France, Russia, Austria and Prussia (by 1914 an important part of Germany) had signed the **Treaty of London**. They guaranteed to protect Belgium's neutrality. A German invasion of Belgium would break the Treaty. Germany would risk war with Britain and France.

On 4 August 1914 German troops poured into Belgium. Only a small Belgian army opposed them. They managed to blow up the railway lines. This cut down the speed of the German advance towards France because it stopped German supplies and reinforcements arriving quickly.

SOURCE **A**

BRAVO, BELGIUM!

This cartoon was published in the British magazine 'Punch' in August 1914.

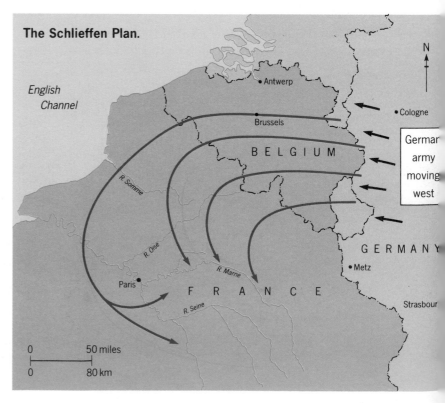

The Schlieffen Plan.

Few British people wanted war. Most believed that because Germany was not directly threatening Britain there was no need to get involved. By 3 August 1914 nearly everyone had changed their minds. This was because of the news that Germany was planning to attack France by invading neutral Belgium. Britain was one of the countries which had guaranteed Belgium's neutrality.

The government decided Britain had to fight. Sir Edward Grey, the Foreign Secretary, convinced Parliament that this was the right thing to do. He told MPs that if Britain did not fight, Germany would win and would dominate Europe. British trade would suffer. Other nations would no longer respect Britain as they had in the past. Grey sat down to thunderous applause. On 4 August the British government sent a telegram to the German government, demanding that German troops should leave Belgium by 11 o'clock that evening. No reply from Germany was received. By midnight Great Britain was at war with Germany.

The country went wild with excitement. Crowds gathered in the streets of London, cheering and singing. It was the same in Paris and St Petersburg, in Berlin and Vienna. Everyone was convinced that their own country was in the right, and that their side would win. Few people knew what they were fighting for, and none guessed at the horrors that lay ahead.

C **SOURCE**

Warm, showers and windy. At work all day. I held a Council at 10.45 to declare war with Germany; it is a terrible catastrophe but it is not our fault. When they heard that war had been declared the excitement (of the crowd outside the palace) increased. The cheering was terrific.

Part of the entry in King George V's diary for 4 August 1914.

British troops leave for war from Victoria Station in 1915.

B **SOURCE**

Activities...

1 Read Source C. King George V wrote that the war was 'a terrible catastrophe'. Why, then, were the crowds cheering?

2 There were many reasons why war broke out in 1914. Here are some of them:
   - Germany wanted an empire
   - Britain wanted the Royal Navy to stay the most powerful in the world
   - Military men in all the Great Powers had made war plans
   - Archduke Franz Ferdinand was murdered in Sarajevo
   Is any one of these reasons more important than the others?

3 Did Britain go to war in 1914 just to defend Belgium? Explain your answer.

3.1 Stalemate

As soon as war was declared, the plans of the Great Powers swung into action. Six hundred thousand German soldiers, packed into railway trains, were already speeding towards Belgium and France. One hundred thousand soldiers of the British Expeditionary Force (BEF) landed at French ports and began marching east. Over one million French soldiers gathered on the German border ready to invade Alsace and Lorraine. Within three weeks everything had gone wrong.

The Schlieffen Plan failed because German troops could not move quickly enough through Belgium into France. The Belgian army fought fiercely, and delayed the Germans for ten days at Liège. The British Expeditionary Force slowed them up still further at Mons. The British plan, which was to stop the German advance altogether, failed. The French Plan Seventeen failed. Three hundred thousand French soldiers were killed or wounded in two weeks as they tried to cross into Alsace and Lorraine.

The German armies pushed on into France. But the Russians mobilized more quickly than expected and invaded Germany from the east. The German commander, von Moltke, ordered troops to the **Eastern Front** to fight them. This left fewer German troops in France. Wearily thousands of German soldiers marched east of Paris towards the river Marne.

Sunday, 9 August 1914
J. Herbert Tritton, Esq. told me his son's regiment – the Coldstream Guards – was under orders, but that his son, Captain Alan Tritton, did not know on what day, or from what station, or from what port, or to what destination the regiment would go.

Notices given out in church: meeting to consider knitting and sewing of garments for soldiers.

An extract from the diary of Rev. Andrew Clark, who was vicar of Great Leighs, Essex.

German troops march to the Marne, September 1914.

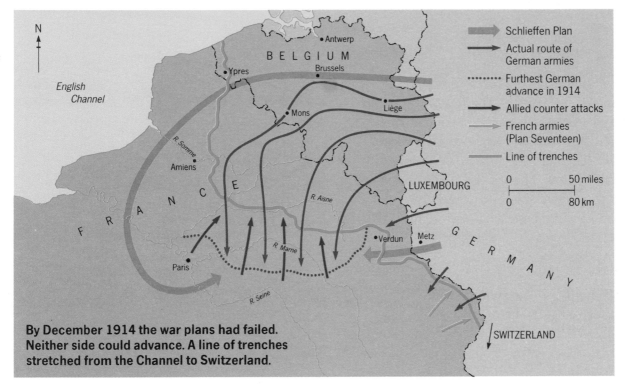

Schlieffen Plan
Actual route of German armies
Furthest German advance in 1914
Allied counter attacks
French armies (Plan Seventeen)
Line of trenches

0 — 50 miles
0 — 80 km

By December 1914 the war plans had failed. Neither side could advance. A line of trenches stretched from the Channel to Switzerland.

French and German soldiers clashed at the river Marne. The German army was trying to advance further into France. French soldiers marched west from Alsace and Lorraine to cut them off. The BEF raced to the river Marne to help the French. The **Battle of the Marne** (5–11 September 1914) was fought fiercely. It was so close to Paris that taxis were able to ferry extra French soldiers to the battle. Gradually the French and British (the Allies) drove the Germans back. By the end of a week the Germans had retreated to the river Aisne. There they dug deep trenches in the ground to protect themselves from enemy fire, and to stop enemy troops advancing any further.

The generals had to think of new plans quickly. Each side tried to **outflank** the other. Terrible battles were fought as the armies raced each other through northern France to the Channel coast. One of these battles was fought around the town of Ypres in October and November 1914. The British and French managed to stop the Germans reaching the Channel ports, but at a terrible cost. Fifty thousand French soldiers, 58,000 British soldiers and 130,000 German soldiers were killed or wounded.

Both sides dug **trenches** to defend themselves and to stop the other side advancing. By December 1914 lines of trenches stretched along the **Western Front** from the English Channel to Switzerland. It was **stalemate**. For the next four years neither side could advance by more than a few miles; savage battles were fought to gain only a few hundred metres of land.

Activities...

1 a List the reasons why the Schlieffen Plan failed.
  b Are all these reasons equally important?

2 Read Source A.
  a Why did Captain Tritton seem to know so little about what his regiment was doing? Was it because:
  • He couldn't remember?
  • He didn't want to worry his father?
  • Army commanders wanted troop movements to be secret?
  b How were people in Great Leighs planning to help British soldiers?

3 Why did soldiers fight from trenches on the Western Front after December 1914?

3.2 Trench Warfare

In the winter of 1914 both sides dug in along the Western Front. They built a complicated system of trenches. The firing trenches were the front line trenches from which attacks were launched. Troops dug short trenches into **No Man's Land**. These led to 'small posts' where one or two soldiers listened carefully for any sign of movement from the enemy. Snipers, too, hid in the 'small posts'. They shot at enemy soldiers.

Behind the front-line trenches were the support trenches and dug-outs. These were more comfortable, and had kitchens, stores and lavatories. Further back still were the reserve trenches, the blacksmiths and stables, tailors and cobblers, field hospitals and the battalion headquarters. Army commanders were far behind the front lines. Communication trenches meant that soldiers could move up to the front line and back again without being seen by the enemy. Messages and orders were carried by runners or pigeons, or were sent by signallers using flags.

Plan of a trench system.

Short trench

To the enemy   No man's land   Small post

Small post
Short trench

Barbed wire

Front line firing trenches

Communication trenches

Company command post

400 metres (approx

Support trenches

Battalion command post

Reserve trenches

Cross-section through a front-line trench.

Barbed wire

No man's land

Sandbags

Elbow rest

Ammunition shelf

Sandbags

2.5 metres

Dug-out

Fire step

Drainage ditch

Duck boards

0.5 metres

SOURCE

'Good-morning; good-morning!' the General said
When we met him last week on our way to the line.
Now the soldiers he smiled at are most of 'em dead,
And we're cursing his staff for incompetent swine.
'He's a cheery old card,' grunted Harry to Jack
As they slogged up to Arras with rifle and pack.

But he did for them both with his plan of attack.

A poem called 'The General' by Siegfried Sassoon, who fought in the 1914–18 war.

The land between enemy trenches was a terrible place. It was pitted with shell holes and littered with abandoned equipment, unexploded shells and rotting bodies which stretcher parties couldn't find. It was called No Man's Land.

The only way to advance on the Western Front was to break through the enemy's trench system. Every battle began with an artillery bombardment, which sometimes lasted for weeks. Huge shells were supposed to destroy the enemy front-line trenches, barbed wire and machine gun posts. After the bombardment, the soldiers were ordered to '**go over the top**' of their trenches and cross No Man's Land to attack enemy trenches. Once out of their trenches the men were easy targets. Thousands and thousands were mown down by machine gun fire.

The problem was, in the early years of the war, that both sides did exactly the same. None of the generals could think of a way to break through the deadlock. All they could do was to carry on with the tactics which their training and experience had taught them would work. Many simply refused to believe the reports of slaughter and disaster they received from the Front. Hundreds of thousands of young men were killed in terrible battles. All that either side ever gained was a few hundred metres of mud.

Activities...

1 What were sandbags, duck boards, fire steps and barbed wire used for?

2 Explain the following:
   • 'go over the top'
   • No Man's land.

3 Why did trench warfare kill so many young men on both sides?

4 Read Source A. What point is Siegfried Sassoon trying to make about soldiers and generals?

5 a What do Source A and Source B together tell you about the Western Front?
   b Are these sources likely to be accurate?

B

SOURCE

Stretcher bearers after the third battle of Ypres at Passchendaele, 1917.

3.3 The Battle of the Somme, 1916

In mid-1915 a 'new' British army began pouring into France. All these men had left their ordinary jobs and had **volunteered** to become soldiers for as long as the war lasted. General Haig (the British commander after December 1915) and General Joffre (the French commander) agreed to use this 'volunteer army' as part of an enormous combined British and French attack against the German lines. The attack was to be made in an area around the river Somme in northern France, and would start in June or early July 1916. The British and French began to equip and train over 100,000 men.

The Germans, however, knew what was happening. Their men in scout planes and observer balloons saw newly-built roads and railway lines, and watched thousands of soldiers arriving with guns, ammunition and supplies. They were not taken by surprise when a massive bombardment began on 24 June. Quickly German troops moved back from their frontline to strongly built dug-outs which were more than 12m deep. On 1 July the bombardment ended. General Haig believed that it had knocked out most of the German front line. He did not know that the Allies had been shelling empty trenches. Haig ordered his troops to advance towards the German lines.

By dusk on 1 July 57,470 Allied and 8,000 German soldiers were dead or wounded. General Haig pressed on. He saw no reason to change his tactics. Between July and November 1916 he ordered attack after attack, always with the same dreadful results. In September, against advice from military experts, he used a new weapon – the tank. Only 50 were ready for war. Twenty-nine of these broke down before reaching the battlefield, and the rest soon got stuck in the mud.

By November both sides were exhausted. Six hundred and twenty thousand Allied and 450,000 German soldiers had been killed or wounded in the **Battle of the Somme**. Of the Allied dead or wounded, 460,000 British soldiers were killed or hurt between July and November 1916. At most the Allies had advanced by 15 km along part of the Western Front.

A SOURCE

The men are in splendid spirits. Several have said that they have never been so instructed and informed of the nature of the operations before them. The wire has never been so well cut, nor the artillery preparation so thorough.

Extract from the diary of General Haig, written on 30 June 1916.

B SOURCE

Quite as many died on the enemy wire as on the ground. The Germans must have been reinforcing the wire for months. It was so dense that daylight could barely be seen through it. How did the planners imagine that Tommies (British soldiers) would get through the German wire? Who told them that artillery fire would pound such wire to pieces, making it possible to get through? Any Tommy could have told them that shell fire lifts wire up and drops it down, often in a worse tangle than before.

Written by George Coppard, a soldier who fought on the Somme in July 1916.

C **SOURCE**

Men of the 2nd Battalion Cameronians (Scottish Rifles) battalion going over the top on 1 July 1916.

D **SOURCE**

At 7.30 am the hurricane of shells ceased as suddenly as it had begun. Our men at once clambered up the steep shafts leading from the dug-outs. The machine guns were hurriedly placed in position. A series of extended lines of infantry were seen moving forward from the British trenches. They came on at a steady pace as if expecting to find nothing alive in our front trenches. A few moments later, when the leading British line was within a hundred yards, the rattle of machine-gun fire broke out. Whole sections seemed to fall. All along the line men could be seen throwing up their arms and collapsing, never to move again.

A German soldier's eyewitness account of 1 July 1916 on the Somme.

E **SOURCE**

British troops at the end of the Battle of the Somme in October 1916. In 1963 A.J.P. Taylor wrote a book called 'The First World War'. He put this photograph in the book and called it 'The rewards of victory'.

Activities...

1 Why did General Haig (Source A) order the attack to begin?

2 **a** In what ways does Source A disagree with Source B?
  b Is General Haig or Private Coppard more likely to have been correct? Explain why you think so.

3 There were 57,470 Allied casualties on the first day of the Battle of the Somme. Which sources best help you to understand why this was?

4 **a** What is a reward?
  b Why do you think Source E is called 'The rewards of victory'?

3.4 Life in the Trenches: Routine

Soldiers on the Western Front did not spend all their time in the trenches. They were supposed to spend four days in front-line trenches, four days in support trenches, eight days in reserve trenches and fourteen days resting. If a battle was taking place, everyone just had to stay put and fight. A battalion of the Black Watch regiment spent 48 days in the front line, before fresh troops could be sent to relieve them.

Night in the trenches was a time of silence and fear. There were patrols in No Man's Land. Men with blackened faces crawled through mud, filth and shell holes trying to spot enemy activity. Sometimes there was a night raid on enemy trenches. All men had to be back in their own trenches before dawn. Once back, an orderly officer checked the trenches, ammunition boxes and stores. Everyone ate breakfast except the sentries, who kept a careful watch. An officer then gave out the day's jobs. One third of the men were put on sentry duty; one third went back for rations, which they brought up the communication trenches to the front line, and the rest worked at such things as repairing the trenches and filling sand bags. At dusk everyone ate an evening meal, and the night-time routine began again.

Soldiers never knew when they would be able to get home on leave. Often it was over a year before they saw their friends and families again. Soldiers longed for 'Blighty', which was army slang for Britain and home. Most of them carried photographs of their families, wives or girlfriends in their tunic pockets. Their only contact with home was by letters and postcards. Soldiers in the front line were allowed to send only field postcards. Those further away from the fighting could write letters. These letters were **censored** by the authorities to make sure that no one had given away information which would help the enemy. Families and organizations like the Red Cross sent parcels of luxuries to the troops – razor blades and soap, cigarettes, cake and chocolate, hand-knitted socks and gloves.

Many men felt that the horrors they lived through could never be fully understood by their friends and families. Their experiences at the Front had changed them. They felt this would cut them off from their old way of life for ever.

SOURCE A

There was always something to be done: digging, filling sandbags, carrying ammunition, scheming against water, strengthening the wire, resetting duck-boards. These duties seemed of such importance that they absorbed one's entire stock of energy.

From 'Up to Mametz', by W. Griffith, 1931. W. Griffith fought with the Allies on the Western Front and wrote about trench life.

SOURCE B

Men were eating, smoking, doing odd jobs, but no one was fighting. I regarded the incessant [continuous] bombardment as temporary and expected every moment to see men going over the top to put the guns out of action. Nothing happened, however. That was how I first saw the war.

From 'Personal Record of the War', by R. Mottram (1929), who fought with the Allies on the Western Front.

A *working party of British soldiers on the Somme in November 1916.*

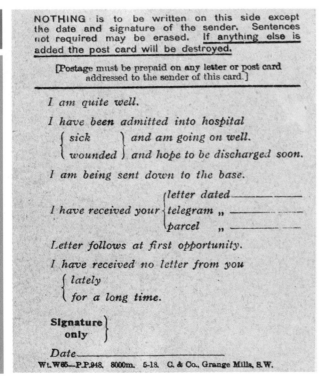

NOTHING is to be written on this side except the date and signature of the sender. Sentences not required may be erased. If anything else is added the post card will be destroyed.

[Postage must be prepaid on any letter or post card addressed to the sender of this card.]

I am quite well.

I have been admitted into hospital
{ sick } and am going on well.
{ wounded } and hope to be discharged soon.

I am being sent down to the base.

I have received your { letter dated _____
{ telegram „ _____
{ parcel „ _____

Letter follows at first opportunity.

I have received no letter from you
{ lately
{ for a long time.

Signature }
only }

Date _____
Wt. W85—P.P.948. 8000m. 5-18. C. & Co., Grange Mills, S.W.

A *British field postcard. This is all the soldiers were allowed to send home. They had to cross out the bits they did not want to say. Some soldiers tried to send secret messages home by crossing out letters to make new words.*

Activities...

1 A lot of trench life was routine. Which of the following might a soldier in the trenches have said?
   • 'I came here to fight, not fill sandbags.'
   • 'I'm bored.'
   • 'I'm kept busy and ready to fight.'
   • 'I'm scared.'
   Which sources did you use to help you decide?

2 Field postcards like Source D did not say much.
   a Why did soldiers want to send them?
   b Why would families want to receive them?
   c Why might the authorities destroy the card?
   d Why did the authorities design a card like this, instead of letting soldiers write what they wanted to?

3.5 Life in the Trenches: Clean and Healthy?

Soldiers in the trenches had to face cold, mud, and the side effects of sleeping rough. In winter, a mug of tea iced over in minutes. Boots froze if they were taken off. The ground in northern France was easily churned into a sea of mud. Men and horses drowned in it. Mud quickly coated boots, socks and trousers, which could not be changed for at least a week. One soldier spent 42 days in 1915 without taking his boots or his tunic off. Regular sleep was impossible.

It was often difficult to get food to troops in the front line. Everything had to be carried along the communication trenches. Mostly the soldiers lived on tinned bully beef (a sort of corned beef) and hard biscuits, bread, margarine and jam. They drank mugs of tea made with condensed milk. Sometimes cheese, bacon and jars of porridge were brought up to the front line. It was only when the men went back down the line that they were able to get regular hot meals from the army field kitchens. All front-line soldiers were given a daily ration of rum early every morning when the night sentries came off duty. Rum was also issued just before an attack to help them make the terrifying leap out of the trenches into No Man's Land.

B SOURCE

The most that could be hoped for was a two-gallon tin (of water) sent up from reserve. This would serve to clean forty men, the last few salvaging what comfort they could from the semi-solid mass. The latrine sap (lavatory) looked so like a mortar position from the air that men preferred to use a pail or helmet and toss the material into No Man's Land. For paper, often a handful of grass or the tail of a shirt would have to do.

From 'Death's Men' by Denis Winter, an historian, 1978.

A SOURCE

British soldiers queue for food at a field kitchen.

C SOURCE

How much food actually arrived in the trenches depended on such things as transport, the weather and enemy action. Wrapping loose rations such as tea, cheese and meat was not considered necessary, all being tipped into a sandbag. In wet weather their condition was unbelievable, and you could bet the rats would get at them first.

George Coppard remembers his life in the trenches.

SOURCE

Your feet swell up two or three times their normal size and go completely dead. You could stick a bayonet into them and not feel a thing. If you are fortunate enough not to lose your feet and the swelling begins to go down, it is then that the agony begins. I have heard men cry and even scream with pain.

A British soldier describes 'trench-foot'.

Men of the Australian Field Artillery in a dug-out at Ypres in 1917.

Soldiers in the front line could not keep clean. They were infested with body lice. Lice lived in warm places on a soldier's body and in his underclothes. They lived by sucking blood. One soldier counted 103 lice crawling around his body and in the seams of his clothes. The only way to kill a louse was by squashing it between thumb and forefinger, or by burning it with a candle or lighted cigarette end. All soldiers hated lice. Second to their hatred of lice was their hatred of rats. The trenches swarmed with them. They fed off left-over food and the rotting bodies in No Man's Land. Flies, too, were a problem. There were 6,000 horses in an infantry division. These horses produced about 40 tons of manure every day, and flies bred in the manure. Soldiers said that sometimes the noise of flies buzzing drowned the noise of the approaching shells; one soldier counted 32 drowning in his shaving water. Flies spread disease.

Trenches were not healthy places. Many soldiers caught colds, 'flu, bronchitis and trench fever, which was spread by lice. Ulcers, boils and impetigo were common, because soldiers scratched lice bites with dirty fingers. The hospital admission list for 1917 shows that thousands of soldiers had dysentery, frostbite, nephritis (a kidney disease), tuberculosis and pneumonia.

Activities...

1 Read Source B.
   a Why were soldiers in the trenches often very dirty?
   b Denis Winter did not fight in the trenches. Can we believe what he writes about conditions there?

2 Field kitchens like Source A meant that soldiers could have hot food regularly.
   a Why were they not used in the front-line trenches?
   b How does Source C help explain why troops in front-line trenches did not have regular meals?

3.6 Life in the Trenches: Casualties

All men at the Front lived with the sight, sound and smell of dead, dying and wounded soldiers. Thousands were killed or wounded in battles, either by shelling or by machine gun fire. Between battles, hundreds more were killed or wounded in trench raiding parties and by snipers.

The fear of death and of the death of friends were two of the worst things a soldier had to live with. Many just could not cope with the horrors they saw every day. Their hands shook and eyes twitched. Some could not hear or speak; others screamed or moaned, and shivered violently whenever guns were fired. This condition was called **shell-shock**. At first sufferers were seen as cowards, but gradually doctors accepted that this was a psychological condition. Men with shell-shock were treated well away from the Front. Some never recovered.

Some soldiers were shot by their own side. This happened to soldiers who ran away. They deserted for many reasons. Some had shell-shock; some were afraid; some had problems at home which they wanted to sort out. They had simply had enough. Many were caught. If they were found guilty of desertion or cowardice, they were shot by a firing squad. During the war, 346 British soldiers were shot in this way.

B

SOURCE

Never before had I seen a man who had just been killed. A glance was enough. His face and body were terribly gashed as though some terrific force had pressed him down, and blood flowed from a dozen fearful wounds. The smell of blood mixed with the fumes of the shell filled me with nausea. Only a great effort saved my limbs from giving way beneath me. I could see from the sick grey faces of the men that these feelings were generally shared. A voice seemed to whisper, 'Why shouldn't you be the next?'

A soldier remembers seeing his first dead body. From 'Death's Men' by Denis Winter, 1978.

A

SOURCE

A badly wounded man is carried through the trenches. He died 30 minutes after this photograph was taken.

C

SOURCE

His steel hat was at the back of his head and his mouth slobbered, and two comrades could not hold him still. These badly shell-shocked boys clawed their mouths ceaselessly. Others sat in the field hospitals in a state of coma, dazed as though deaf, and actually dumb.

A soldier describes 'shell-shock'. From 'Eye Deep in Hell' by J. Ellis, 1976.

Part of a painting called 'An Advanced Dressing Station at the Front', painted by Henry Tonks in 1918. He was a British artist who had once been a surgeon. In 1917 he was sent to the Western Front as an official war artist.

At night, after a battle, stretcher parties searched No Man's Land for wounded soldiers. Some of the wounded made it back to their own front line; others were hurt in the trenches. All needed help quickly. While it was still dark the wounded men were taken back down the line, through the communication trenches. Regimental medical officers gave first aid in specially built shelters. They tried to sort out which soldiers needed a sling or a bandage and could later be sent back to the Front, and which needed further treatment.

Soldiers who were seriously injured were sent to Casualty Clearing Stations. These were mobile hospitals situated several kilometres behind the lines. Only the heaviest artillery shelling could reach them. They were therefore reasonably safe. Doctors and nurses worked hard. They had to decide which soldiers had to be operated on there and then, and which soldiers were too ill to be moved. These men stayed at the Casualty Clearing Stations. The others were taken, sometimes by train, to base hospitals. There the soldiers were cared for until they were well enough to fight again. Some soldiers were sent home to hospitals and nursing homes in 'Blighty'. Many, however, died of their wounds or from infection.

Activities...

1 Look at Source A. Why is the wounded man being carried on another man's back, and not on a stretcher?

2 Read Source B. What does it tell you about a soldier's attitude to death?

3 What is shell-shock? Use Source C to help you explain.

4 Look at Source D.
  a What happened in field hospitals?
  b Source A is a photograph. Source D is a painting. Which is more reliable as a source of evidence?
  c Why would the British government want to send official war artists to the Western Front?

4.1 The British Empire

All the people in the British Empire were subjects of King George V. Most of them believed that the war Britain was involved in was their war too. They did what they could to help. The countries of the Empire sent men, money and materials to help fight Germany and Germany's allies.

Australia, Canada, India, South Africa and New Zealand sent thousands of soldiers to fight with troops from France and Great Britain on the Western Front. They fought in other countries too. **Anzacs** (soldiers from Australia and New Zealand) set up a garrison in Egypt. They also captured German colonies in New Guinea and Samoa. Anzacs fought fiercely, too, at **Gallipoli** where they were part of a plan to invade Turkey and bring help to Russia. The plan was disastrous. Nearly half the Anzacs were killed or wounded. Indian troops helped to make the Gulf oil supplies secure, and were involved in capturing Mesopotamia (now Iraq). South African soldiers concentrated on attacking German colonies in Africa, and captured German South West Africa. By the end of the Great War, over 200,000 men from the Empire had been killed and more than 600,000 injured.

The Empire gave Great Britain other kinds of support. For example, India helped solve some land transport problems. The Indian government sent over 100,000 animals, including elephants, to the Middle East. Three thousand Australian munitions workers came to work in British factories.

The vast resources of the British Empire helped make Britain and its allies hard to beat.

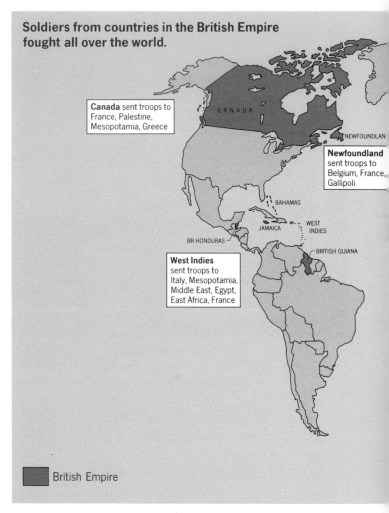

Soldiers from countries in the British Empire fought all over the world.

Canada sent troops to France, Palestine, Mesopotamia, Greece

Newfoundland sent troops to Belgium, France, Gallipoli

West Indies sent troops to Italy, Mesopotamia, Middle East, Egypt, East Africa, France

British Empire

A SOURCE

Soldiers from the British West Indies Regiment cleaning their guns on the Albert to Amiens road in Northern France, September 1916.

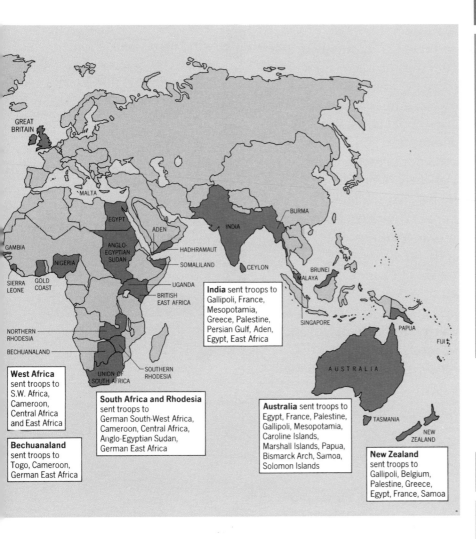

West Africa
sent troops to
S.W. Africa,
Cameroon,
Central Africa
and East Africa

Bechuanaland
sent troops to
Togo, Cameroon,
German East Africa

South Africa and Rhodesia
sent troops to
German South-West Africa,
Cameroon, Central Africa,
Anglo-Egyptian Sudan,
German East Africa

India sent troops to
Gallipoli, France,
Mesopotamia,
Greece, Palestine,
Persian Gulf, Aden,
Egypt, East Africa

Australia sent troops to
Egypt, France, Palestine,
Gallipoli, Mesopotamia,
Caroline Islands,
Marshall Islands, Papua,
Bismarck Arch, Samoa,
Solomon Islands

New Zealand
sent troops to
Gallipoli, Belgium,
Palestine, Greece,
Egypt, France, Samoa

A poster displayed in India during the Great War. The caption says 'Give money to help our warriors'.

A poster used in Australia during the Great War.

Activities...

1 Look at Sources B and C.
  a What are they asking for?
  b How is each poster trying to get its message across?

2 Explain how soldiers from Australia and India helped Allied forces fighting in the Great War.

3 The British Empire was spread throughout the world.
  a How did this help Britain fight the Great War?
  b How could this cause problems for Britain?

4.2 Allies and Enemies

In August 1914 an army of 800,000 Russians smashed into Germany. The German army stopped them at **Tannenberg** and at the **Masurian Lakes**. The slaughter was terrible. Three hundred thousand Russians were killed or wounded. Throughout 1915 German and Austrian armies advanced steadily into Russia. The Russian army could not stop them. They did not have enough guns, ammunition and food. The Russian road and railway system could not take the strain. Military commanders, led by the Tsar, were often incompetent. Throughout 1916 and 1917 starving Russian soldiers, many of them horribly wounded, tramped home. Their anger turned against their leaders; many thought of revolution.

In 1915 **Italy** joined the war on the side of Britain and France. The Italian army fought fiercely, often in deep snow high up in the mountains. They made little progress. In October 1917 the Austrians, with some crack German troops, began an advance at **Caporetto**. The Italian army fled, retreating 70 miles in seven days. This left many Italians feeling angry and ashamed.

A

SOURCE

The sight of thousands of Russians driven into two huge lakes to drown was ghastly and the shrieks and cries of dying men and horses I will never forget. To shorten their agony (the Germans) turned their machine guns on them. Five hundred men on white horses, all killed and packed so closely together that they remained standing, was the ghastliest sight of the whole war.

An eyewitness account by a German officer, writing in 1914.

Alliances during the Great War.

- Entente Powers at outbreak of war
- Countries that later joined the Entente Powers
- Central Powers at outbreak of war
- Countries that later joined Central Powers
- Neutral throughout the war

Turkey joined the war on the side of Germany. This made problems for Britain and France. Now they could not help Russia by getting supplies in through the Black Sea. The Gallipoli campaign, which had tried to win a route through, was a disaster. Turkey could also threaten the Suez Canal and Britain's position as protector of Egypt. It might be able to stop vital oil supplies getting to Britain and France from the Persian Gulf. Britain quickly looked for allies. The Arabs lived in part of the Turkish Empire. Britain promised them a free homeland if they would fight with the Allies. A guerrilla army of Arabs, led by an English colonel, T. E. Lawrence, attacked Turkish supply routes. This weakened the Turkish forces and the British army was able to capture Baghdad, Jerusalem and Damascus. The Turkish army was destroyed by General Allenby in September 1918. The British never kept their promise to the Arabs.

Japan was the first non-European country to join the war. Japan had made an alliance with Britain in 1902. Twelve years later, when war was declared, Japanese troops invaded China and seized German colonies there. They also captured the Caroline and Marshall islands in the Pacific ocean. All through the war, Japanese battleships protected Allied troop carriers and supply ships in the Pacific Ocean.

As you have seen, a quarrel between Austria and Serbia turned into a general European war. This European war quickly became a world war because the Great Powers had empires and alliance networks which spread throughout eastern Europe, Asia and the world.

Our tent was made with tarpaulin drawn over petrol cans. A bunch of dirty Arabs came down the pass on camels. Their leader in his white headdress spoke: 'My name is Lawrence. I have come to join you'. On our journey he told me of the difficulties. We had three methods of progress – to bluff, buy or fight our way through.

A British soldier remembering his time spent serving in the Middle East.

Activities...

1 What can you find out about German and Russian soldiers from Source A?

2 a Why was Turkey a problem for Britain?
  b How did T. E. Lawrence help?

3 How can you tell, from Sources B and C, that fighting conditions in the Middle East were different from those on the Western Front?

4 The Great War began in Europe. How did it turn into a world war?

Hospital riverboats moored on the waterway Shatt el Arab in Mesopotamia (now Iraq) in 1917.

4.3 The War at Sea

In 1914 the Royal Navy was the strongest in the world. Britain relied on the navy to keep the seas clear of enemy ships. Vital supplies of food and raw materials could then be brought into Britain. Troops could be moved to where they were needed. When war broke out the Royal Navy tried to stop the German **High Seas Fleet** from putting to sea. They blockaded German ports. This also stopped merchant ships entering German ports with supplies.

Several ships from the German navy were at sea when war was declared. Some of them became raiders, attacking merchant ships which carried supplies for Britain. The German raider *Emden* captured over 20 merchant ships before it was sunk in November 1914. The whole German **Pacific Fleet** was destroyed at the Battle of the Falklands a month later.

Britain did not want to risk a major North Sea battle unless it was really necessary. If Germany won, Britain would have lost control of the sea. The Germans tried to lure the Royal Navy into action. German ships shelled Hartlepool, Whitby, Scarborough and Great Yarmouth. There were minor battles at Heligoland (1914) and Dogger Bank (1915). Then in 1916 the German Admiral Scheer ordered the High Seas Fleet into the North Sea. This was serious. On 31 May both fleets met off Denmark in the **Battle of Jutland**. Britain lost more ships and more men than Germany. This was probably because the British ships had only thin armour around their gun turrets. However, the German fleet suddenly stopped fighting.

A SOURCE

British battleships 'Orion', 'Thunderer', 'Monarch' and 'Conqueror', built in 1912. They were all at Jutland and all survived.

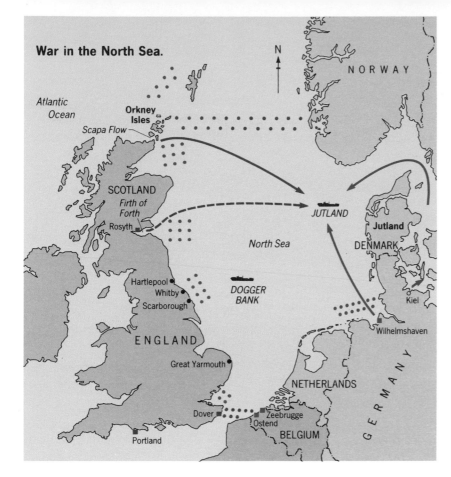

War in the North Sea.

- • • • • British minefields
- • • • • German minefields
- ■ British naval bases
- ■ German U-boat bases
- • Towns shelled by German navy
- ⚓ Naval battles
- → German Fleet (Von Scheer)
- → Grand Fleet (Jellicoe)
- – → Battle Cruiser Fleet (Beatty)

| 0 | 200 miles |
| 0 | 300 km |

During the night both fleets headed for home. The German High Seas Fleet never left port again. Britain remained in control of the North Sea.

Both sides used **submarines**. Germany built large numbers of *Unterseeboten*, nicknamed **U-boats**. U-boats attacked and sank merchant ships. In May 1915 the U-20 torpedoed the passenger liner *Lusitania* which was sailing from New York to Liverpool. Over 1,000 passengers were drowned, among them 124 Americans. People in America were very angry, even though the liner was carrying war materials as well as passengers. The German Kaiser was afraid the USA would join the war against Germany. He ordered U-boat warfare to be cut back.

In January 1917 Germany began all-out submarine warfare again. The plan was to starve Britain of raw materials and food. It seemed the only way to win the war. They very nearly succeeded. In March and April, one ship in every four leaving a British port was sunk. There was only enough food left in Britain to feed everyone for six weeks. The Prime Minster, David Lloyd George, decided that merchant ships should sail in large groups protected by fast destroyers. This convoy system cut merchant shipping losses from 25% to 1%. Britain did not starve and did not surrender.

D **SOURCE**

German shipyards were switched from building surface ships to building submarines. German sailors were taken off their ships and trained for submarine warfare. German admirals drew the lesson from their failures of 1916 that an unrestricted submarine campaign was their decisive card.

From 'The First World War' by A. J. P. Taylor, 1963.

Activities...

1 Use Sources A, B and the map.
   a Where had Churchill sent the fleet?
   b Why did he want its whereabouts kept secret?

2 Read Source D. Why was Germany so keen to build submarines?

3 Why were there no great sea battles in the Great War?

4.4 The War in the Air

A British naval airship guards a convoy.

In 1914 no one knew whether aeroplanes would be any use in the war. The first plane had flown only 11 years earlier. The Great Powers had only a few hundred planes each. These were mostly made of wood and canvas, held together with piano wire. Cockpits were open and pilots had to wear layers of warm clothes, thick gloves, leather helmets and goggles to stop themselves freezing to death in the air. There were few instruments; engines were unreliable and there were no parachutes. It needed courage to fly a plane, let alone fight in one.

The Royal Flying Corps sent 41 planes and some observation balloons to France with the British Expeditionary Force. These were to be the 'eyes' of the army. They flew high above the enemy lines and reported back on such things as troop movements, trench systems and ammunition dumps. They were particularly useful during a battle. They could advise whether the enemy was attacking or retreating. The Royal Naval Air Service (RNAS) were the navy's 'eyes'. They reported on the movement of enemy ships, and helped to protect ships on their own side. The RNAS used airships a lot. They could travel longer distances than planes without refuelling.

B SOURCE

The first time I saw a German machine both the pilot and myself were unarmed. We waved a hand. The enemy did likewise. This did not seem ridiculous. There is a bond of sympathy between all who fly – even enemies.

A British airman remembers the war.

C SOURCE

I know that I shall meet my fate
Somewhere among the clouds above;
Those that I fight I do not hate,
Those that I guard I do not love …

Nor law, nor duty bade me fight,
Nor public men, nor cheering crowds,
A lonely impulse of delight
Drove to this tumult in the clouds;
I balanced all, brought all to mind,
The years to come seemed waste of breath,
A waste of breath the years behind
In balance with this life, this death.

From 'An Irish Airman Foresees his Death', by W. B. Yeats.

Most of the first airmen were armed with revolvers or machine guns. Sometimes they had bombs which they dropped over the sides of their cockpits. Gradually planes developed into fighting machines. Antony Fokker, a Dutch engineer working for the Germans, invented a mechanism which meant that airmen could fire through the blades as the propeller went round. The Allies used a system of fighter planes flying in formation to protect their spotter and bomber planes. They made bombing raids on enemy airports, railways and supply depots. Planes on both sides fired on troops in the trenches.

Dog-fights in the sky between fighter planes were common over the Western Front. Air aces became heroes. The number of enemy planes they shot down were known like test match scores or football results. There was René Fonk (75); Mick Mannock (73) and Baron von Richthofen (80). For most pilots reality was different. By 1916 many were boys aged 18, who were given a brief training and sent into battle. They could expect to live for three weeks. By 1918 the Great Powers were, altogether using over 10,000 planes in the front line, and over 50,000 airmen had been killed.

Part of a painting by G. H. Davis showing a dog-fight.

Activities...

1 How did the Royal Flying Corps help the British Expeditionary Force?

2 Why was the airship (Source A) of more use than a plane?

3 a British and German airmen were enemies. Why then, according to Source B, did they wave to each other?
  b In what ways do Sources B and C agree?
  c Sources B and E were both written by airmen. Why do they seem to disagree so much?

4 What can a painting like Source D tell you that a photograph cannot? What problems might there be in using a painting as historical evidence?

Two machines jump up before me. A couple of shots. Gun jammed. I feel defenceless and in my rage I try to ram an enemy's machine. The guns begin to fire again. I see the observer and pilot lurch forward. Their plane crashes in a shellhole. The other Englishman vanishes.

From the memoirs of a German airman.

5.1 Artillery and Machine Guns

SOURCE

A

A British howitzer in action on the Somme.

B

The real test was the barrage. Some hid their heads in their great-coats. Some wept; others joked hysterically. But all shook and crawled, white faced in dull endurance. 'How long? How long?' men would ask themselves again and again. Men had no choice but to last out, nerves pared to the bone.

From 'Death's Men' by Denis Winter, 1978.

At the start of the war, all the Great Powers used mobile field guns. These fired about six rounds a minute and were fairly accurate. They were not, however, a lot of use once both sides were dug into trenches along the Western Front. Larger and more powerful guns were developed to bombard enemy lines. The largest of all was made by Germany. It was nicknamed 'Big Bertha' and could fire a 108 kg shell a distance of 132 km. It was aimed at Paris.

Artillery bombardment of enemy trench systems was not reliable; this tactic went badly wrong at the Battle of the Somme (see page 16). Later in the war new tactics were adopted; the artillery was used to protect the soldiers as they advanced. Sometimes this 'creeping' barrage went wrong too, and the artillery ended up shelling its own troops. A bombardment, or barrage, was meant to destroy enemy defences. Some barrages also destroyed roads, bridges, and railways. Sometimes whole villages and even towns would disappear.

C

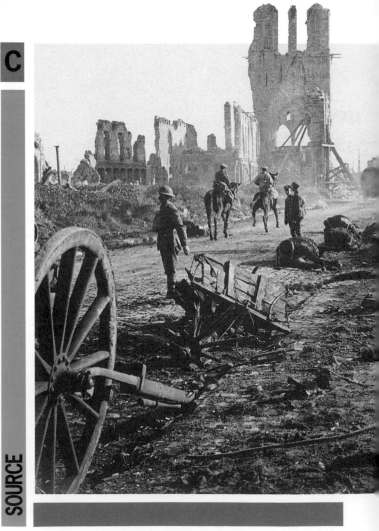

A town after an artillery bombardment in 1917.

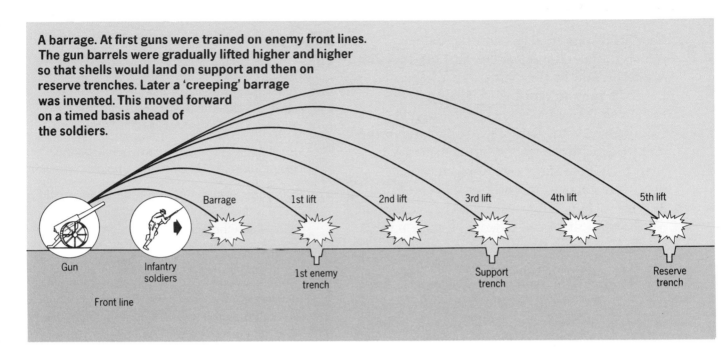

A barrage. At first guns were trained on enemy front lines. The gun barrels were gradually lifted higher and higher so that shells would land on support and then on reserve trenches. Later a 'creeping' barrage was invented. This moved forward on a timed basis ahead of the soldiers.

There was stalemate on the Western Front because both sides dug themselves into trenches which they defended fiercely and successfully. All men were equipped with high velocity bolt action repeating rifles and hand grenades. But for many soldiers, the two most important weapons on the Western Front were shovels and machine guns. They used shovels to dig the trenches which protected them from snipers' fire and shrapnel. They used machine guns to defend their trenches. The problem was that both sides did the same.

Direct attack on an enemy's front-line trenches seemed like suicide. Soldiers moving slowly across open ground were easy targets for machine gunners. Whole battalions were mown down in this way. The smoke and noise of the battlefield separated men from their commanders. Orders were often lost. Senior commanders, usually miles away from the trenches, often refused to accept that battles were not going the way they planned.

D

SOURCE

Whatever the nature of weapons used on the Western Front, the men who carried them were trapped in a war of futility and monumental suffering, the origins of which lie not in guns but in the minds of the men who sent them there.

From 'The Experience of World War One' by J. M. Winter, 1988.

Activities...

1 Sources B and C describe some results of bombardments. What were these results? Were they meant to happen?

2 Look at the diagram and explanation of a creeping barrage. How could artillery end up shelling their own side?

3 Read Source D.
   a Is J. M. Winter saying that men died for nothing because their weapons were useless, or because the generals' tactics were useless?
   b Is J. M. Winter giving us facts or opinions about the past? How can you tell?

5.2 Gas and Tanks

New ideas were tried to break the stalemate of trench warfare. Poison gas was first used on the Western Front by the Germans at the Second Battle of Ypres in April 1915. Hundreds of French and Algerian soldiers suffocated in thick chlorine gas. Canadians were gassed later in the month, and British troops for the first time in May. Soon both sides were using chlorine, phosgene and mustard gas. Gas suffocated and blinded soldiers. They feared and hated mustard gas the most. It caused hideous blisters on the skin and ate away slowly at men's lungs.

Gas was a terrifying but unreliable weapon. In damp weather the gas would drift around at knee height; if the wind changed direction troops could end up gassing their own side. A gas alarm system was developed in the trenches, and soldiers were given gas masks. These worked quite well, provided the troops could get them on quickly enough. Soldiers who were only lightly gassed recovered their sight and breathed easily after a few hours. Others were blinded for life, or had their lungs so badly damaged that they never fully recovered. All troops remembered the terror and panic of gas attacks.

B SOURCE

Gas! Gas! Quick, boys! – An ecstasy of fumbling,
Fitting the clumsy helmets just in time;
But someone still was yelling out and stumbling
And flound'ring like a man in fire or lime…
Dim, through the misty panes and thick green light,
As under a green sea, I saw him drowning.

In all my dreams, before my helpless sight,
He plunges at me, guttering, choking, drowning.

If in some smothering dreams, you too could pace
Behind the wagon we flung him in,
And watch the white eyes writhing in his face,
His hanging face, like a devil's sick of sin;
If you could hear, at every jolt, the blood
Come gargling from the froth-corrupted lungs,
My friend, you would not tell with such high zest
To children ardent for some desperate glory,
The old Lie: Dulce et decorum est
Pro patria mori.*

* It is sweet and proper to die for one's country. Part of a poem by Wilfred Owen called 'Dulce et Decorum Est'. Owen fought in the trenches and was killed on 4 November 1918, just seven days before the war ended.

British soldiers after a gas attack.

A SOURCE

SOURCE

A Mark IV tank which belonged to the 1st Battalion, British Tank Corps. The huge bundle of sticks above the cab is called a fascine. The fascine could be rolled out like matting in front of the tank and helped it to cross wide trenches. The diagram below shows how the crew of eight fitted into the tank. They had to work in hot, cramped conditions.

Inside a Mark IV tank.

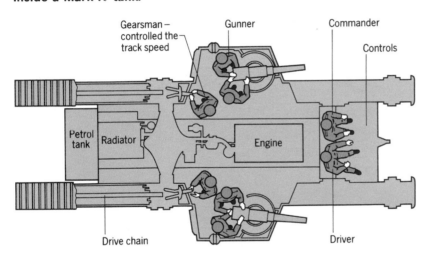

SOURCE

It would be wrong to claim that tanks won the war, but they did provide an answer to the stalemate of trench warfare.

From 'The Experience of World War One' by J. M. Winter, 1988.

Activities...

1 Gas was an unreliable weapon. Why did both sides use it?

2 a What do Sources A and B tell you about gas attacks?
  b Which source is more likely to be reliable? What makes you think so?

3 Tanks were slow and clumsy; soldiers working in them were hot and uncomfortable and some went mad. Why, then, were they used at all?

4 What sources would J. M. Winter have used to help him reach the conclusion he did in Source D?

Another attempt to break the stalemate of trench warfare was the tank. A British army journalist, Lt-Colonel Ernest Swinton, designed an armed vehicle which could cross difficult ground. After trials in Britain with a variety of tractors, 50 tanks made their appearance at the battle of the Somme. They were not a success (see page 16). It was a different story in November 1917. At the Battle of Cambrai more than 400 Mark IV tanks smashed their way through the German trenches. In three days they had driven 8 km behind the German lines. The German High Command believed that to use tanks was to admit that all proper military tactics had failed. German field commanders, however, were happy to use captured British tanks. German development work was slow, and German tanks did not come into service until March 1918, when it was almost too late.

6.1 Recruitment and Conscription

When war was declared thousands of men volunteered to join the 247,000 regular soldiers in the British army. Many believed that the war would by over by Christmas, and they were anxious not to miss it. Many wanted a chance to fight for their country. **Lord Kitchener**, the Secretary of State for War, told the government that he would need an army of millions to defeat Germany. The government began a recruiting campaign to persuade even more young men to volunteer.

Recruiting offices opened in almost every town and city. Speakers at rallies talked about the better world which would follow victory, and whipped up hatred against the Germans. Women handed out white feathers to men in civilian clothes they suspected were too afraid to join up. Hundreds of posters, books and pamphlets were distributed up and down the country. The campaign was so successful that army barracks were overflowing and there were not enough rifles to go round. Friends joined up together: whole football teams, young men from the same back-streets, factory floors and offices. They were trained together, usually by elderly officers and sergeant-majors, in 'Pals' battalions. Many 'Pals' battalions were almost wiped out at the Somme. Some villages and towns lost almost all their young men on the same day. People never imagined it would be like this.

B SOURCE

I had a dead end job in a dead end town. Here was a chance to see the world.

From 'Personal Memories' by Alfred Blake.

C SOURCE

I feel I am meant to take an active part in this war. It is to me a very fascinating thing, something if often horrible, yet very ennobling and very beautiful.

From 'Testament of Youth' by Vera Brittain, 1933. The book is about her early life. Roland Leighton is explaining to his fiancée, Vera Brittain, why he has volunteered to fight.

D SOURCE

I thought we would have a good time, have a good adventure, it was supposed to be over by Christmas 1914, what a joke.

Oliver Powell, a miner from Tredegar in South Wales, explains why he joined up.

A SOURCE

Volunteers for Lord Kitchener's Army, London 1914.

By March 1916, 2.5 million men had volunteered to join 'Kitchener's Army'. There was, however, a growing feeling in Britain that thousands of young men were getting out of fighting. The government decided to introduce **conscription**. In 1916 the first Military Service Act was passed by Parliament. This forced all unmarried men aged 18–41 to join the services. Later in 1916 it was extended to include married men.

Men whose conscience would not allow them to fight were known as **conscientious objectors**. They could appeal to a tribunal which decided whether or not they had to be made to go to the Front. Some men were sent to non-fighting duties like ambulance work; others were sent to work camps. Many claims were rejected and objectors were sent to the Front. When they refused an officer's order, they were court martialled and either shot or sent home in disgrace.

SOURCE **E**

We've watched you playing cricket
And every kind of game:
At football, golf and polo
You men have made your name.
But now your country calls you,
We shall love you all the more.
So come and join the forces
As your fathers did before.

Oh, we don't want to lose you,
But we think you ought to go,
For your King and your Country,
Both need you so.
We shall want you and miss you,
But with all our might and main
We shall cheer you, thank you, kiss you,
When you come back again.

A First World War recruiting song.

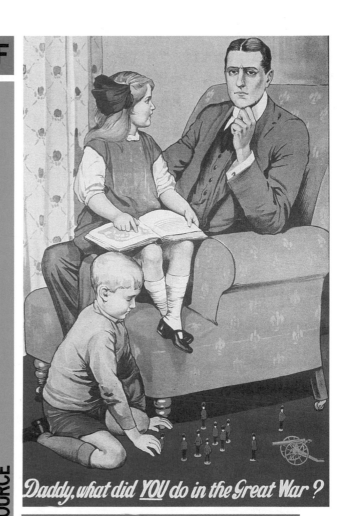

SOURCE **F**

A First World War recruiting poster, issued by the government.

Activities...

1 a What different reasons did the men in Sources B–D give for joining Kitchener's Army?
  b What other reasons might men have had?

2 a Explain how the song (Source E) and the poster (Source F) tried to persuade men to join up.
  b Which do you think would have been the most successful, and why?

3 How useful would sources A–F be if you were trying to find out about recruitment between 1914 and 1918?

6.2 Factories and Farms

The government had to be sure that the men at the Front had all the supplies they needed. Everything, from bullets to boots, from shells to sandbags had to be made and sent out from Britain. The government therefore took control of factories, mines and transport. They had the power to do this because of a new law called the **Defence of the Realm Act** (DORA). It was the first time a British government had this power.

There were fewer men to work at home in industry and on the land. Workers were urgently needed in the munitions factories, to keep trains and buses running and to do office work. Women had to be employed. Many men felt threatened. Some thought that women would work for less money and so take their jobs from them; others thought that a woman's place was at home. The government made special arrangements with the trades unions for this 'dilution' by women. It was agreed that women workers could replace skilled men for wartime only. When the men returned, the women would have to give up their jobs. Many women who went to work in the factories were better paid than they had been in domestic service. For the first time they were having the same sort of freedom as men.

B SOURCE

They didn't want to show us their livelihood. You see, they knew it was their livelihood. Women were coming in, you see. They were going to cut the wages.

Part of an interview recorded by Elsa Thomas just after the war. She went on a training course at Woolwich Arsenal, a munitions factory in London.

C SOURCE

1 February 1916
Today the men from Lang's on the Clyde are out on strike owing to the introduction of women into the works.

An extract from Frances Stevenson's diary. She was secretary to David Lloyd George, who was Prime Minister from December 1916 to October 1922.

D SOURCE

Some of the labourers on the Wolds (an area of Lincolnshire) who were not used to their wives going out said that the same standard of comfort and cleanliness was impossible in their homes under the new conditions.

From a report 'Wages and Conditions of Employment in Agriculture', 1919.

A SOURCE

Women workers at Vickers Ltd, May 1917. They are doing skilled precision machine work, turning brass nose cones for shells.

In 1914 Britain had the largest merchant fleet in the world. Ships took coal, textiles and manufactured goods all over the world. The goods they brought back included important basic foodstuffs like wheat from Russia and the USA, and meat from Australia and Argentina. British farmers were unable to compete with this cheap imported food. By 1914 80% of the wheat needed by Britain was imported. 50% of the milk, fruit and vegetables eaten and drunk by British people came from abroad. In times of peace and prosperity this did not matter. In wartime it mattered very much. In 1914 the government bought in bulk supplies of wheat and sugar. They made special arrangements for the supply of jute from India (needed for sandbags) and flax from Russia (needed for tent canvas).

By the autumn of 1916 Britain was growing short of food. German U-boats had stopped most supplies getting in. The government began food rationing. Sugar, butter, meat and tea were all rationed. Bread was not. The government then tackled the main problem, which was that not enough food was being produced in Britain itself. They persuaded farmers to plough up rough land. They fixed minimum rates of pay for farm labourers to encourage them to stay on the land. They persuaded women to join organizations like the Women's Land Army to work on farms. By 1918 three million extra acres of land were being cultivated; the potato crop had increased by 1.5 million tons and wheat by one million tons.

Government poster, 1917.

Activities...

1 **a** What do Sources B–D tell you about the way men felt about women working?
   b Do you think it likely that all men felt the same? Why?

2 Now look at Source A. Does this source prove that men were right to be afraid that women would take their jobs? Explain your answer.

3 Which of Sources A–D best shows the problems made by the agreement between the government and trades unions that women could 'dilute' the workforce? Give reasons for your answer.

4 Look at Source E.
   a What is the government trying to persuade people to do?
   b What does the government hope will happen as a result?

6.3 Transport and Finance

The government had to make sure that raw materials got to the munitions factories making bullets and shells, and to all the other factories and workplaces which were making things like boots and tents which were needed by the troops. It also had to make sure that the finished goods got from the factories to the ports for shipping to the Front. It was not only freight that had to be moved. Men who had volunteered to fight, or had been conscripted (see pages 36–37) had to be moved from training camps to ports so that they could join the war. In order to do this efficiently, the government decided they had to take over the railway system. In 1914 they set up a Railway Executive Committee. This controlled and co-ordinated the whole network of 140 separate railway companies. The work of the REC was made even more difficult because 700 engines and 20,000 wagons were sent to the Western Front.

The government controlled the railways, but this did not, by itself, mean that the railways could be run efficiently. Railways needed coal to power the engines and people to run the rail network. In 1914 thousands of coal miners volunteered to fight. When conscription was introduced (see page 37) the government had control over who went to fight. Many miners were told that they had to spend the war years mining coal. This was as important as fighting. Over 50,000 women were taken on by the railways to work as porters and clerks, telephonists, signal operators and ticket collectors. By 1918 the railways carried 50% more freight than in 1914.

A SOURCE

Defence of the Realm Act

NOTICE

The continuance of traffic on the railways is necessary for the safety of the nation and for the prosecution of the war. Any person who prevents or attempts to prevent another person from working on a railway at the present time is liable to six months imprisonment.

Copy of a notice put up by the Chief Constable of Staffordshire in August 1917.

B SOURCE

A woman railway worker operating signals on the Great Central Railway, Birmingham, in September 1918.

SOURCE

A government poster published during the First World War.

BACK·HIM·UP BUY WAR BONDS

Wars are expensive, and they have to be paid for. In 1916 it was calculated that the war cost £3.85 million every day. The money had to be found somewhere. About 70% of the cost of the war was paid for by government borrowing. The rest came from the pockets and bank balances of British people. The government raised income tax from 9*d* (3.75p) in the pound in 1914 to 6/- (30p) in the pound in 1918. In 1914 1.5 million people paid **income tax**; by 1918 this had risen to 7.75 million. The government set up a scheme for people to buy **war bonds** from them. At the end of the war the money spent on the bonds would be returned to them, plus interest. For the government it was a way of borrowing money; for many people it was a way of saving. The banks helped the government too. Before 1914 anyone could take a banknote into a bank and ask for it to be changed into gold. This was stopped during the war. The Bank of England printed more money than it had gold in its strongrooms. No gold left the country. The government could use it if there was a desperate emergency.

D

SOURCE

The aim was to win, no matter what the cost. Therefore the main economic priority was to produce the necessary quantity of goods to defeat the enemy.

From 'The Economic Effects of Two World Wars on Britain' by A. S. Milward, 1984.

Activities...

1 How do Sources A and B **together** show how important the government thought the railways were at this time?

2 a How is the government trying to persuade people to buy war bonds in Source C?
  b Now look back at Source E on page 39. Which of the two posters do you think would have been better at persuading people to do what the government wanted? Why?

3 Read Source D. Which of the sources you have seen so far in this part of the book support what A. S. Milward wrote?

6.4 Propaganda

Between 1914 and 1918 the government had to make sure it had the support of the British people in fighting the war. It had to persuade young men to fight and die; to convince women that their husbands, sons and fathers should go to war; to encourage people at home to work and go without in order to support the war effort.

Governments of all the Great Powers used **propaganda** to persuade people; to tell them what to think and to convince them that it was right to fight. The British Government wanted people to believe that the Germans were wicked monsters who did terrible things to innocent people. Newspapers printed what the government wanted people to read. Posters and pamphlets carried government messages. Some of the information given out was partially true; some of it was total lies. The government believed it could not tell the whole truth because people would begin to question whether it was worth fighting at all.

B A 'Corpse Conversion' factory
A peep behind the German lines

Out of their own mouths, the military masters of Germany stand convicted of an act of unspeakable savagery by improvising a factory for the conversion of corpses into fat and oils, and fodder for pigs. How was the discovery made? Quite simply. Herr Karl Rosner, the Special Correspondent of the Berlin 'Lokalanzeiger' on the Western Front, made the announcement in his published dispatch of 10 April.

SOURCE

From a government Department of Information pamphlet, 1917.

A TAKE UP THE SWORD OF JUSTICE

SOURCE

A government recruiting poster, 1915.

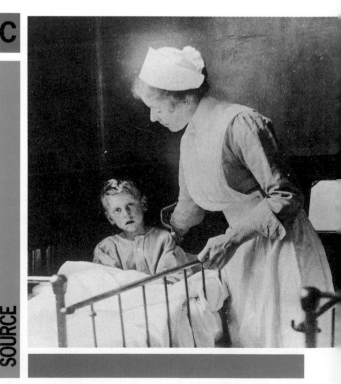

C

SOURCE

Many photographs were taken of injured children and distributed by the government.

D

Four frames from a cartoon film, made for the government, shown in cinemas at the beginning of 1918.

E

A government poster distributed in 1914.

Activities...

All of these sources were made to try to persuade people to think and behave in certain ways.

1 For each source, say:
  a What the government wanted people to believe.
  b How it was trying to make them believe this.
  c What the government hoped people would do.

2 Sources A, B and E did not tell the whole truth:
  • **Source A**: When the *Lusitania* was sunk by the German submarine U-20 in 1915, it was carrying a cargo of ammunition for British bases
  • **Source B**: In 1925 it was admitted in the House of Commons that this story was a lie
  • **Source E**: No one ever saw a German nurse do this in front of prisoners
  a Why did the government not tell the whole truth at the time?
  b Would it have made any difference if they had?

3 The sources in this unit are all examples of propaganda. Does this mean that they are no use to historians?

7.1 Food and Drink

In 1914 there were about 45 million people living in Great Britain. A lot of the food they ate came from abroad (see page 41). War meant food shortages. Not only did German U-boats sink ships bringing food to Britain, but the government had to make sure that supplies went abroad to feed the troops. Shops ran out of food like meat, eggs, butter and margarine. Some people began hoarding food. Prices rocketed. The government Food Controller tried to make sure that food was fairly distributed around the country. This did not always work, and people grew angry about shortages, high prices, and the hours they had to spend queueing for food. Women doing war work in munitions factories, on the buses and elsewhere could not queue for food for their families. Some of them bought hot meals from one of a string of national kitchens set up by the Ministry of Food, and took them home to eat. Others ate in new cost-price restaurants set up by various charities. However, a bad winter and increased U-boat activity meant that there was very little food in Britain by spring 1917. The government had to start food rationing. In April meat was rationed; by the summer so was tea, sugar, butter, margarine and lard. Local committees controlled the supply of things like tea, jam and cheese, and the price of bread and potatoes was set by the government. Food queues vanished, and most people had just about enough to eat.

B

Saturday 24.2.1917
2.20pm afternoon's post brought me: a circular from the Food Controller urging all ministers of religion to encourage a voluntary cut-back in food consumption to avoid rationing. Suggested limits were four pounds of bread, two and a half pounds of meat and three-quarters of a pound of sugar per head per week.

From the diary of the Rev. Andrew Clark, vicar of Great Leighs, Essex.

C

My daughter went out at 7am to the Maypole Dairy Co. shop and after waiting till 10.30am was turned away without any margarine, came home chilled to the bone besides losing her education. If we could have a system of rationing, I believe these hardships could be overcome.

A letter to a newspaper 'The Workers' Dreadnought' 19 January 1917.

A

Protests against the price of milk, 1916.

Before the War, public houses in London were open from 5am to 11pm. Outside London they opened from 6am to 10pm. Men and women could drink as much as they liked when they liked. There were over 3,300 convictions a week in 1914 in England and Wales for drunkenness. In April 1915 a report on timekeeping in the shipping, munition and transport industries was published. This said that people were turning up late for work, or not turning up at all, because they had been drinking too much. The war effort was suffering. The government therefore amended the Defence of the Realm Act, (DORA) so that they could control the drink trade. Pubs' opening times were cut to just two and a half hours in the middle of the day, and two to three hours in the evening. Some towns made it harder for women to buy drink. In Plymouth women could not buy drinks after 6pm although men could buy them until 9pm. In London women, unlike men, could not buy a drink before 11.30am. Beer was watered down. The price was put up from 3d to 9d (1.25p to 3.75p) a pint, and the cost of spirits increased 500%. These changes meant that ships crossing the Atlantic did not have to carry so much grain for brewing, but could carry other goods.

D SOURCE

THE ENEMY'S ALLY.

A cartoon published in the magazine 'Punch' in 1915.

Activities...

1　**a** What was the Rev. Clark (Source B) asked to do?
　b How would this make a difference to the lives of people in his parish?

2　Why did some people want rationing and others oppose it? Use Sources A, B and C to help you in your answer.

3　What is the connection between
　• the amendment to DORA to include trade in alcoholic drinks;
　• ships crossing the Atlantic;
　• the British war effort?

E SOURCE

We are fighting Germany, Austria and drink, and, as far as I can see, the greatest of these deadly foes is drink.

Part of a speech made by David Lloyd George in Spring 1915.

7.2 Bombs, Spies and Invasion

On 19 January 1915 two German airships, called zeppelins, appeared over the east coast of England. These giant balloons, shaped like a cigar and over 190m long, were a beautiful silvery colour. No one on the ground knew why they were there. One hovered over Great Yarmouth. For a few moments nothing happened. Then for ten minutes bombs fell on the town. Two people were killed and many houses damaged. Nothing like this had happened before. The second airship bombed King's Lynn. Then they both turned back to Germany. Four months later zeppelins raided London for the first time. In all they made 54 raids on British towns, killing 557 people and injuring many more. No one had ever thought Britain would have to be defended from air attacks. Soon anti-aircraft guns were built, searchlights installed and barrage balloons set up. The zeppelin threat was over.

Worse was to come. In May 1917 German Gotha bombers raided Folkestone and killed 95 people. The following month they bombed London. One hundred and sixty two people were killed, including sixteen children who died when their school was bombed. Gotha bombers made over 27 attacks on British towns. For the first time ordinary people were being killed and injured in their houses, shops and offices. War was not just for the soldiers at the Front.

Mrs Holcombe Ingleby, wife of a Conservative MP, describes a zeppelin raid on London in August 1915. She wrote this in a letter to her son who was an army officer in Cairo.

Sybil Morrison describes what she felt when she saw the first zeppelin shot down.

A **SOURCE**

Territorial soldiers clearing up after a zeppelin raid on King's Lynn, 19 January 1915.

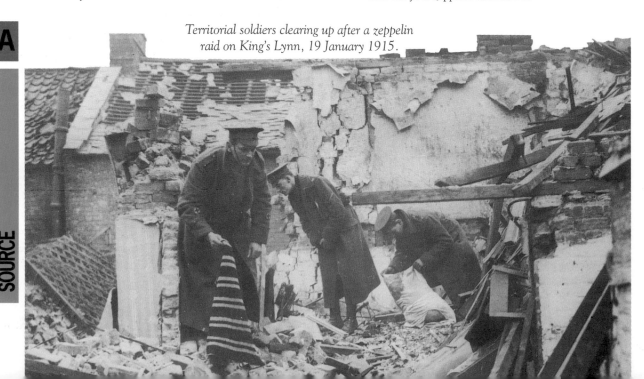

It was not only zeppelins and bombers that attacked British towns. In the first months of the war ships from the German navy crossed the North Sea. They fired shells at Hartlepool and killed 119 people including babies. They shelled Scarborough and Whitby too. People began to believe that the Germans were preparing to invade Britain. They didn't know how well or badly the war was going because the government censored all the news. So many people believed nearly every story they heard about German spies, plots and invasion. Some of the stories were incredible. Nearly everyone knew someone who knew somebody who had seen Russian soldiers marching south from Scotland – with snow on their boots!

Some people in authority took the danger of invasion very seriously indeed. Special constables were appointed. One of their jobs would be to tell British people what to do if the Germans landed. The Lord Lieutenant of Lincolnshire issued a proclamation which told people what to do when the Germans invaded. Copies were kept secret and returned once there was no danger of invasion. Everyone kept a look out for spies, and told each other the latest rumour. Some people were very afraid.

D

SOURCE

Friday 30.10.1914
Sir Richard Pennyfather told how the spy hunt at Little Waltham had been fully justified by a recent event. One wet evening his men had found a man sheltering beside a haystack; they had seized him but found no bomb or fire raisers. When Sir Richard and his motor had gone, pent-up merriment broke forth. It was comic that a man in authority should be ignorant of the common tramp and his habit on wet nights of sleeping rough.

From the diary of the Rev. Andrew Clark, vicar of Great Leighs, Essex.

E

SOURCE

Sea Scouts helped the coastguards. This Sea Scout is checking that the man has a permit for taking photographs on the seashore.

Activities...

1 a Read Source B. What did Mrs Holcombe Ingleby feel as she watched the zeppelin?
  b Now read Source C. What did Sybil Morrison feel as she watched the zeppelin?
  c Why do you think the two women had such different attitudes to zeppelins?

2 Look at Source A. Do you think that either Mrs Holcombe Ingleby or Sybil Morrison would have felt differently if they had lived in King's Lynn?

3 Why did people react so differently to the threat of invasion? Use the information on page 46 as well as Sources D and E to help you answer the question.

7.3 Attitudes

Many Germans lived and worked in Britain, and had done so for years. However, once war was declared, a lot of British people became suspicious of foreigners living in their midst. Many believed government propaganda about German atrocities. They turned on the Germans.

Workers went on strike in factories employing Germans. There were demonstrations against German traders and professional men still working openly. German food was taken off menus in restaurants; shopkeepers refused to stock sauerkraut and German sausages. The Royal Family changed its surname from the German 'Saxe-Coburg-Gotha' to 'Windsor'. Other people with German-sounding names did the same. Children even threw stones at dachschund dogs. After the sinking of the *Lusitania* mobs attacked and looted shops owned by Germans in Manchester, Liverpool, London and other cities. Only a few of the rioters were arrested, and they were given very small fines.

The government decided to **interne** all foreign men, including Germans, who were old enough to fight. They were taken away from their jobs, friends and families and put in camps until the war ended.

SOURCE A

An anti-German riot in High Stret, Poplar, in the East End of London in May 1915.

SOURCE B

Rioting was going on quite near here. It is a mercy that they have interned the Germans at last. It ought to have been done long ago. It is a pity that our folk descended to lawlessness, but it was the only way our people could show their feelings in the matter. We have a great camp of German prisoners of war (soldiers) not far from here. Would you believe that some people were actually asking for *cakes* for them!

Part of a letter from Margaret Lilley, of Stroud Green, London. It was written in May 1915.

Women workers at a clothing factory in London with German prisoners of war. The factory made uniforms for German prisoners of war in Britain and British prisoners of war in Germany.

All sides in the war took prisoners. The British sent their German prisoners to live in camps in various parts of Great Britain. These camps were sometimes buildings like old schools and workhouses which were no longer needed. Sometimes they were specially built. Most prisoners worked, under guard, outside the camps during the day. They worked on building sites and on the land. They all wore specially made uniforms so they could be spotted quickly if they tried to escape.

D

Monday 4 March

The German prisoners are hard at work on the aerodrome at Chelmsford. They have quarters in the Workhouse and are marched back there from their work about 4.30pm each day. They are said to be very happy, laughing and joking with each other as they pass along the street. Several Chelmsford girls have been taken before the magistrates for giving them stamps and chocolate.

Thursday 29 August

Mrs Matthew has four German prisoners doing work on her farm. They are brought in a lorry at 8 am. They have a meal at the Chelmsford Workhouse before they start in the morning, and bring another meal with them. She does not think this is enough, because they work until 7 or 8pm. She is annoyed because the authorities forbid her giving them more food, but quietly ignores the prohibition. The men are excellent workers.

From the diary of the Rev. Andrew Clark, vicar of Great Leighs, Essex.

Activities...

1 The Germans living in Britain during the war had many different experiences. Describe the different experiences of
   • the owner of the shop in Source A
   • the prisoners of war in Source C.

2 Look at Source A and read Source B. Did Margaret Lilley agree with what the looters were doing?

3 Read Source D. Why did the girls from Chelmsford and Mrs Matthew help the German prisoners of war, even though they knew they were breaking the law?

7.4 War Poetry

There are a lot of poems about the First World War. Most of the poems were written at the time, and by men who fought in the trenches and battlefields. Many of the poets were killed. All of the poets were trying to tell us of their feelings about the War. Some of the verses on these two pages are complete poems; others are verses from longer poems. There are poems on other pages in this book, too. They tell us what the poets felt about the War. They also tell us what the poets wanted us to know about the War.

For the Fallen

They went with songs to the battle, they were young,
Straight of limb, true of eye, steady and aglow.
They were staunch to the end against odds uncounted:
They fell with their faces to the foe.

They shall not grow old as we that are left grow old:
Age shall not weary them, nor the years condemn.
At the going down of the sun and in the morning
We will remember them.

Written by Laurence Binyon (1869–1943). He was in charge of Oriental paintings at the British Museum during the Great War.

The Soldier

If I should die, think only this of me:
That there's some corner of a foreign field
That is for ever England. There shall be
In that rich dust a richer dust concealed;
A dust whom England bore, shaped, made aware
Gave, once, her flowers to love, her ways to roam,
A body of England's, breathing English air,
Washed by the rivers, blest by suns of home.

Written by Rupert Brooke (1887–1915) between November and December 1914. Rupert Brooke died on the way to Gallipoli in 1915.

Returning, We Hear the Larks

Sombre the night is.
And though we have our lives, we know
What sinister threat lurks there.

Dragging these anguished limbs, we only know
This poison-blasted track opens on our camp –
On a little safe sleep.

But hark! joy – joy – strange joy.
Lo! heights of might raging with unseen larks.
Music showering on our upturned faces.

Death could drop from the dark
As easily as song –
But song only dropped . . .

Written by Isaac Rosenberg (1890–1918). He fought and was killed in the Great War.

Breakfast

We ate our breakfast lying on our backs
Because the shells were screeching overhead
I bet a rasher to a loaf of bread
That Hull United would beat Halifax
When Jimmy Stainthrope played full-back instead
Of Billy Bradford. Ginger raised his head
And cursed, and took the bet, and dropped back dead.
We ate our breakfast lying on our backs
Because the shells were screeching overhead.

Written by Wilfrid Gibson (1878–1962). He fought in the Great War and survived.

The Dug-Out

Why do you lie with your legs ungainly huddled,
And one arm bent across your sullen, cold,
Exhausted face? It hurts my heart to watch you,
Deep-shadow'd from the candle's guttering gold;
And you wonder why I shake you by the shoulder;
Drowsy, you mumble and sigh and turn your head . . .

You are too young to fall asleep for ever;
And when you sleep you remind me of the dead.

Written by Siegfried Sasson (1886–1967), an officer who fought in the Great War and survived.

Does it Matter?

Does it matter – losing your legs? . . .
For people will always be kind,
And you need not show that you mind
When others come in after hunting
To gobble their muffins and eggs.

Does it matter? – losing your sight? . . .
There's such splendid work for the blind;
And people will always be kind,
As you sit on the terrace remembering
And turning your face to the light.

Do they matter? – those dreams from the pit?
You can drink and forget and be glad,
And people won't say that you're mad,
For they'll know you've fought for your country
And no one will worry a bit.

Written by Siegfried Sassoon.

You smug-faced crowds with kindling eye
Who cheer when soldier lads go by,
Sneak home and pray you'll never know
The hell where youth and laughter go.

Written by Siegfried Sassoon.

If any question why we died,
Tell them, because our fathers lied.

Written by Rudyard Kipling (1865–1936). His son was killed in the Great War.

Futility

Move him into the sun –
Gently its touch awoke him once,
At home, whispering of fields unsown.
Always it woke him, even in France,
Until this morning and this snow.
If anything might rouse him now
The kind old sun will know.

Think how it wakes the seeds, –
Woke, once, the clays of a cold star.
Are limbs, so dear achieved, are sides,
Full-nerved, – still warm – too hard to stir?
Was it for this the clay grew tall?
– O what made fatuous sunbeams toil
To break earth's sleep at all?

Written by Wilfred Owen (1893–1918). He fought in the Great War and was awarded the Military Cross. He was killed one week before the war ended.

Activities...

1 *Returning*, *We Hear the Larks*, *Breakfast* and *The Dug-Out* are all about day-to-day routines.
   What does each poet say to make these routines frightening?

2 *For the Fallen*, *The Soldier* and *Futility* are about death.
   Why do the three poets say such different things about the same subject?

3 In *Does it Matter?*, what is Siegfried Sassoon's attitude towards disabled soldiers and the people with whom they lived after the War?

8.1 At the Front

It was not only men who went to the Front. Between 1914 and 1918 over 25,000 women worked behind the front lines in Europe, Asia and Africa. At first the British government did not want women, apart from nurses, to work anywhere near the fighting. As the war went on, more and more men were needed to fight. The government reluctantly agreed to allow women to do things like drive ambulances. The men who were doing these jobs were sent to fight.

Most of the women who went to the Front belonged to some sort of organization. Women in the First Aid Nursing Yeomanry (FANYs) and the Voluntary Aid Detachment (VADs) helped overworked nurses and men in the Royal Army Medical Corps. By September 1916 there were over 8,000 VADs working in military hospitals. The women were not paid for the work they did, and therefore most of them came from upper and middle-class families who could support them. Vera Brittain was the daughter of a wealthy Staffordshire manufacturer. She was at Oxford University studying for a degree when she decided to join the VADs. She nursed wounded and dying soldiers in France. Her fiancé, Roland Leighton (see Source C on page 36) was killed in France. So was her brother Edward.

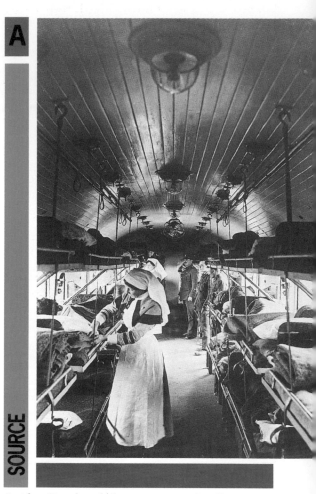

A SOURCE

Inside a British ambulance train near Doullens, northern France, 27 April 1918.

The Women's Auxiliary Army Corps (WAAC) was a different sort of organization. WAACs were recruited from all classes, and were paid wages for the work they did. They worked behind the front lines as cooks, drivers, mechanics, telephonists and clerks.

B SOURCE

The train came from the Front into Calais station. The doctors came round with the list of how many vacant beds there were and they labelled the men with the hospital to which they had to go. Then we drivers had to go in and find our own labels. For a long time we had to carry our own men out to the ambulance.

Beryl Hutchinson, who was a FANY, remembers what it was like being an ambulance driver.

C SOURCE

We received requests for stores from the Front line. They came all on a list, and we had to divide it up and send it to the various departments – depots they were called – clothing to one group, and guns, heavy guns, light guns and so on.

Ruby Ord remembers what it was like working for the WAAC as a Field Indents clerk at Calais.

The women who went to France, particularly those from well-off families, found living conditions very different from those at home. Most lived in hostels, Nissen huts or tents. There was never enough water, so they could not keep themselves clean. They had to face rats, fleas, lice and bugs of all sorts. The women faced the same dangers as the men: they could be killed, wounded, gassed or taken prisoner.

Elsie Knocker and Mairi Chisholm set up a dressing station which operated from a bombed-out cellar. It was just 14 m behind the front line at Pervyse in Belgium. They cared for injured and dying men from the moment they were hurt. Elsie and Mairi were both badly gassed. King Albert of the Belgians personally gave them the 'Order of Leopold' to honour their bravery. Edith Cavell also worked in Belgium. She was a Red Cross nurse, and looked after British, Belgian and German soldiers. She also helped British soldiers escape. The Germans found out. They court-martialled her and shot her.

E

SOURCE

We eventually arrived at Etaples. Our camp was composed of Nissen and long wooden huts. I was allocated a bed along with about 19 other girls. The beds were composed of hard mattresses and a pillow and two rough dark blankets. Each morning before going to work we had to fold the blankets and place them with the pillow at the bottom of the bed. It wasn't very comfortable sleeping without sheets.

A member of the WAAC remembers what it was like to live in a camp in northern France.

Activities...

1 a What were FANYs, VADs and WAACs?
 b What were the differences between them?

2 a How did women's lives change when they went out to the Front?
 b Twenty-five thousand women went out to the Front. Would all their lives have changed as much and in the same way?

D

Women air mechanics of the Women's Royal Air Force (WRAF) working on the fuselage of an Avro bi-plane. The Women's Royal Air Force began in April 1918; the Women's Royal Naval Service (WRNS) started five months earlier in November 1917.

SOURCE

8.2 Back Home

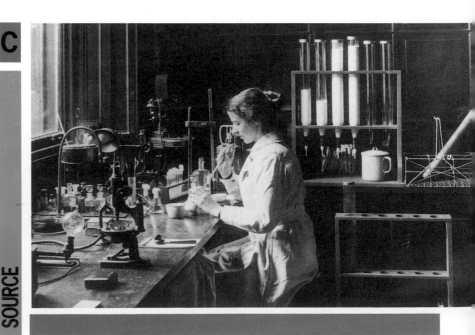

A SOURCE

I was born in a small village called Four Mile Bridge, near Holyhead, Anglesey – one of a family of eleven – seven girls and four boys – myself being the second daughter. My father was a blacksmith, working hard to keep his large family. During the Great War there were no strikers to make the horses' shoes, so at the age of sixteen I did all the striking, and between us we managed to keep the Smithy open. At the time I was studying for my matriculation at the Holyhead Grammar school, which meant that the horses' shoes had to be made very early in the morning before cycling the five miles to the school. We usually managed to make eight shoes and father could then get on with the shoeing during the day.

Mrs J. C. Teare remembers helping her father keep his blacksmith business running while she was a schoolgirl during the First World War.

Not all the work done by women in 1914–18 was directly aimed at winning the war. Many worked to keep factories and family firms going until the men returned. Women worked, for example, in the Govan shipyards of Harland and Wolff on the Clyde; at the Glasgow Gas works; in the flour mills of Rank and Sons at Birkenhead. They worked in breweries, tanneries, linoleum factories, caustic soda works and for window cleaning firms. Most women then went home to look after their families single-handed, because the men had left to fight in the war.

B SOURCE

This married woman took over her husband's chimney sweeping business while he was away fighting.

Most women supported the war. They cared for their families while the men were away fighting; they took men's jobs in offices, factories and on the land; they worked at the Front; they persuaded their husbands and brothers to fight, and supported those who were at the Front.

C SOURCE

Woman working in a bacteriological laboratory in Glasgow, 1918.

D SOURCE

The Women's Peace Conference held at The Hague in 1915.

E One woman, enclosing £10, says, 'I have lost one son in the war, and another is in the trenches. Thank God that at last the women are waking up.' Four soldiers' wives clubbed together to send 10s (50p), saying they have not known peace of mind since the ghastly slaughter started.

From a newspaper report about the letters which were pouring in to the Appeal launched by the Women's Peace Crusade.

Some women were opposed to the war. In 1915 over 1,000 of them from twelve different countries met at The Hague, in the Netherlands, to discuss how the war could be ended. They called themselves the 'Women's International League for Permanent Peace'. When they got home to their own countries the women set up branches of the 'Women's International League'. By 1918 there were almost 5, 000 members in Britain. Most were upper and middle-class women living mainly in London and Manchester. They published pamphlets, leaflets and held meetings to try to persuade other women to support them.

Some women wanted to do more. They formed the Women's Peace Crusade, and held huge meetings and rallies in towns and cities like Leicester, Nelson and Manchester. Thousands of women marched with them. Children carried banners saying 'I want my Daddy'. A lot of people were very angry about this. They tore down posters and broke up meetings. Even so, by 1918 there were 120 branches of the Women's Peace Crusade up and down the country.

Activities...

1 Read Source A.
   a How had the war changed this girl's life?
   b Not everything in her life changed. What things stayed the same?

2 Now look at Sources B and C. What do you think might have changed in these women's working lives, and what would have stayed the same?

3 **a** In what ways did women help the war effort?
   b How different were the women who joined the Peace Crusade?

9.1 The Final Offensive

By the beginning of 1918 people had had enough of the war. Most families had lost someone in the fighting. Everyone was affected by shortages of food, clothes and fuel. In January there was a strike of 100,000 workers on the Clyde; by July there were widespread strikes throughout the country. To make matters worse, Spanish 'flu, which was raging in Europe, reached Britain and killed 151,446 people within a year.

The men at the Front were equally disillusioned. By the end of 1917, 150,000 men had died in the **Battle of Passchendaele**. All that had been gained was five miles of land around Ypres. Soldiers were beginning to hate the generals, and to wonder what they were fighting for. However, in April 1917 news came that the USA had declared war on Germany. Many hoped that when large numbers of fresh, well-equipped American troops reached Europe, they would make all the difference.

The German Kaiser and the German High Command realized that their best chance of winning the war had come. War against the Russians on the Eastern Front ended in 1917. Germany could now concentrate its troops along the Western Front where they would outnumber the Allied forces. However, Germany had to attack before Austria-Hungary, Bulgaria and Turkey collapsed in the east; before the starving German people forced the army to give up, and before thousands of American troops arrived in Europe. On 21 March 1918 the German attack began. British troops were pushed back over the Somme battlefield. Thousands surrendered. The Germans advanced 60 km into France.

A SOURCE

As the dreary summer of 1918 drew to a close and autumn set in, it seemed as though the war would last until there were no more men left to fight.

A woman who lived through the war wrote this about 1918.

B SOURCE

The man in the ranks is no longer aware of why he is fighting. He has lost both faith and enthusiasm.

Douglas Haig, Commander-in-Chief of British forces, said this in 1918.

C SOURCE

MILITARISM

THE SANDS RUN OUT.

A British cartoon published in 1918.

After five months the German troops were exhausted. Too many men had gone too far, too fast. Then the Allies hit back. American troops began to arrive in early summer. The counter-attack began in August. The British used 456 tanks to spearhead an attack in the north at Amiens. Further south the French and Americans fought fiercely, and the Belgians attacked at Ypres. The final battle began on 26 September. The Allies captured the Hindenburg Line (the strongest German trenches) and took 400,000 prisoners. The German army collapsed. In the east, Germany's allies, Bulgaria, Austria-Hungary and Turkey were all defeated. Inside Germany, ordinary people were close to despair. Thousands were starving. Hundreds died every day from Spanish 'flu. Riots were common, and there was talk of revolution. The German government wrote to the American President, Woodrow Wilson, and asked for an armistice. On 11 November 1918, in a railway carriage in the French forest of Compiègne, the German government agreed to the Allies' demands. At 11.00am all fighting stopped. The Great War was over.

D SOURCE

Over there, over there,
Send the word, send the word over there,
That the Yanks are coming, the Yanks are coming,
The drums rum-tumming everywhere.
So prepare, say a prayer,
Send the word, send the word to beware.
We'll be over, we're coming over,
And we won't come back till it's over, over there.

An American song, written by G. M. Cohen in 1917.

E SOURCE

Once the Americans were in, the result was almost certain to be a German defeat. The United States had vast supplies of manpower and materials, far greater than the Germans could achieve. Germany fast became exhausted; so too did Britain and France – but they could be boosted by America.

From 'War in the Trenches' by M. Holden, 1973.

Activities...

Chuck and Annie are talking about the First World War.

Chuck: The Americans really won the war. The British were exhausted. They had been fighting since August 1914. They couldn't win by themselves. The USA joining in on the side of the Allies made all the difference. American troops were going to stay in Europe until the war was over. They were going to win.

Annie: What rubbish! Germany's last chance to win the war came early in 1918. Germany very nearly won. They pushed the Front 60 km into France and shelled Paris. They lost because the Germans used the wrong tactics. The Americans had nothing to do with it.

1 We all use a mixture of facts and opinions when we talk to each other. Read what Chuck and Annie are saying. For each of them, list the facts and the opinions they use.

2 Chuck and Annie say different things about the part played by the USA in the Allied victory. Do you think this is because there are some things Annie does not know about American involvement?

3 Where did Chuck get his ideas from?

4 From what you have read, do you agree with Chuck or Annie?

9.2 Armistice Day: 11 November 1918

The Armistice which ended the Great War was signed at 5 o'clock in the morning of 11 November 1918. The Great Powers agreed to stop fighting at 11 o'clock that morning. The news travelled rapidly to politicians and people in cities like London, Paris, Vienna and Berlin as well as to the troops at the Front. Most people wanted the war to end. Their reactions to the end of the war were, however, very different.

The front page of the 'Daily Mirror' newspaper, 12 November 1918.

The crowds cheered and sang as they flocked to Buckingham Palace. The King comes out on to the balcony: 'With you, I thank God and rejoice' he tells them, and whether they can hear his words or not they cheer and cheer and cheer again. Strangers join hands and sing 'God Save the King' and 'Rule Britannia'. Out in Trafalgar Square the crowd is dancing, singing again the songs of the war. 'Have we won the War?' is roared and an answering roar comes, 'Yes, we've won the War'.

A woman remembers 11 November 1918.

Abergavenny, 18 November 1918
There was not any great excitement in any place where I go on account of the war finishing. They got bands out and organized marches but the people generally, while they seem glad that the end is arriving, don't have the heart to demonstrate much.

Mr Price in a letter to his son, who was a conscientious objector and in prison.

SOURCE D

The 18th Battalion Australian Imperial Force, on 11 November 1918, listening to their Commanding Officer announcing the signing of the Armistice.

SOURCE E

Already this was a different world from the one that I had known during four life-long years, and in this brightly lit, alien world I should have no part. All those with whom I had really been intimate were gone; not one remained to share with me the heights and depths of my memories. As the years went by and youth departed and remembrance grew dim, a deeper and ever deeper darkness would cover the young men who were once my contemporaries. The war was over; a new age was beginning; but the dead were dead and would never return.

Vera Brittain, who worked as a VAD in France, remembers her feelings on Armistice Day.

SOURCE F

He would not be killed. No one in the battalion would be killed. Incredible. Then he thought of the millions of men of many nations who were gone for ever, rotting in desolate battlefields and graveyards all over the world. He turned his head further from the men to hide the tears which, to his amazement, came into his eyes. Would they dare to maffick (celebrate wildly) in London and Paris? Probably. Well, let them. Perhaps the men's quietness and lack of demonstration meant that they too felt this. The only victory that had resulted was in fact the victory of death over life, of stupidity over intelligence, of hatred over humanity. It must never happen again, never, never.

David Jones writes about the feelings of officers and men on 11 November 1918 in 'In Parenthesis', 1938.

Activities...

1 Sources A–F are about people's reactions to the Armistice. For each source, say what the person concerned felt about the end of the war.

2 Why do you think these people reacted so differently to the end of the war?

10.2 Losses

Nearly 750,000 British servicemen were killed in the First World War. Hundreds of thousands more were injured. Most of those who died were young men aged between 18 and 25. Their deaths were tragedies for their families. They also had terrible long-term effects. Children grew up without fathers; widows grew old without husbands; young women stayed unmarried and childless all their lives. The men who died, or who were horribly injured, could have grown up to be talented doctors, designers, engineers, engine drivers, plumbers, poets, or politicians. Many people call them the 'lost generation'.

A

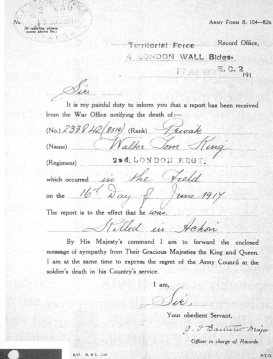

Army Form B. 104—82a.

Territorial Force   Record Office,
4 LONDON WALL Bldgs.
17 Jul 1917   E.C.2   191

Sir,

It is my painful duty to inform you that a report has been received from the War Office notifying the death of:—

(No.) 2338 42 (8519) (Rank) Private
(Name) Walter Tom King
(Regiment) 2nd. LONDON REGT.
which occurred in the Field
on the 16th Day of June 1917
The report is to the effect that he was

Killed in Action

By His Majesty's command I am to forward the enclosed message of sympathy from Their Gracious Majesties the King and Queen. I am at the same time to express the regret of the Army Council at the soldier's death in his Country's service.

I am,
Sir,
Your obedient Servant,
J. F. Bartlett Major
Officer in charge of Records

Letters like this were sent to the families of people who had been killed or injured.

B

SOURCE

King George V presenting war widows with their dead husbands' medals.

C

SOURCE

Over 240,000 servicemen had leg or arm amputations, like these men.

D

SOURCE

I can remember my mother going pale one afternoon as she saw the telegram boy coming towards the house. She turned to me and smiled as he cycled past, but she didn't say a word. My father and brother were in the navy, and you never knew if the telegram was for you.

A woman remembers what it was like in the war when she was 14 years old.

WAACs looking after the graves of dead British soldiers at Etaples in France. This photo was taken in 1919. A few years later the wooden crosses were replaced by white headstones. The graveyards are still there. They are looked after by the Commonwealth War Graves Commission.

The government decided that it wanted a lasting memorial to those who had died in the war. In 1920 the body of an unknown soldier was brought from France. With pomp and ceremony he was buried in Westminster Abbey. A flame burns always by his grave. He represents all those who died in the First World War.

What have we the living to say to the dead who pass by in shadowy hosts? They died that the world might be a better and cleaner place for those who lived and for those who came after. As that unknown soldier is borne down Whitehall he will issue a silent challenge to the living world to say whether it was worthy of his sacrifice. And if we are honest with ourselves, we shall not find the answer easy.

A journalist wrote this after watching the procession taking the Unknown Warrior to Westminster Abbey.

Act, Defence of the Realm 38, 45
Act, Military Service 37
airships 30
Alsace and Lorraine 6, 10, 12, 13
Amiens 57
Anglo-Japanese Alliance 27
Anzacs 24
Asia 27, 52
Asquith, Herbert 61
Australia 24, 25, 39, 59
Austria-Hungary 6, 8, 9, 27, 56

Baghdad 9, 27
Balkans 7, 9
barrage 32, 33
base hospitals 23
Battles: Cambrai 35
    Caporetto 26
    Dogger Bank 28
    Falklands 28
    Heligoland 28
    Jutland 28
    Liège 12
    Marne 13
    Masurian Lakes 26
    Mons 12
    Passchendaele 56
    Somme 16, 19, 32, 35, 36, 56
    Tannenberg 26
    Ypres (2nd) 34
Belgium 10, 12, 53
Berlin 9, 11, 58
Big Bertha 32
Binyon, Lawrence 50
Black Hand 9
Blighty 18, 23
bombardment 15, 16, 32
British Empire 6, 24
British Expeditionary Force 10, 12, 13, 30
Brittain, Vera 36, 52, 59
Brooke, Rupert 50
Bulgaria 9, 56

casualty clearing stations 23
Cavell, Edith 53
Cenotaph 5
Churchill, Winston 28
conscientious objectors 37
conscription 37, 40
convoys 29, 30
Coppard, George 16, 20
court martial 37, 53

Damascus 27
desertion 22
dilution 38

Earl Haig Fund 4
Eastern Front 12, 56
Egypt 24, 27
Entente Cordiale 7

factories, munition 38, 40, 44, 49, 60

feathers, white 36
field hospitals 14
    kitchens 20
firing squad 22
First Aid Nursing Yeomanry 52
Flanders 5
Fleming, Alexander 60
Fokker, Antony 31
Fonk, René 31
France 6, 7, 10, 11, 12, 13, 16, 24, 26, 27, 53, 56
Franz Ferdinand 8
Franz Joseph 6

Gallipoli 24, 27
General Allenby 27
General Haig 16, 56
Germany 6, 7, 9, 11, 24, 26, 27, 28, 29, 32, 36, 56
Great Britain 6, 7, 11, 24, 38, 39, 44, 49
Great Powers 7, 10, 12, 27, 30, 31, 32, 42, 58

Imperial Airways 60
income tax 41
India 24, 25, 39
internment 48
Italy 7, 26

Japan 27
Jerusalem 27

Kaiser Wilhelm II 6, 7, 9, 29, 56
King George V 11, 24, 62
Kipling, Rudyard 51

Lawrence, TE 27
Leicester 55
Leighton, Roland 36, 52
Liverpool 29, 48
Lloyd George, David 28, 45
London 5, 11, 45, 46, 48, 55, 58
Lord Kitchener 36

machine guns 15, 22, 31, 32
Manchester 48, 55
Mannock, Mick 31
Middle East 24
Ministry of Food 44

national kitchens 44
navy, German 28, 29, 47
navy, Royal 6, 28
Nelson, Lancs. 55
New Zealand 24
No Man's Land 14, 15, 18, 20, 21, 23

observer balloons 16, 30
Ord, Ruby 52
Owen, Wilfred 34, 51

Paris 11, 13, 58
Persian Gulf 27

planes 16, 30, 31, 46, 47
Plan Seventeen 10, 12
poppies 4, 5
postcards, field 18, 19
Princip, Gavrilo 8, 9
prisoners of war 52

Railway Executive Committee 40
Red Cross 18, 53
Rev. A. Clark 12, 44, 47, 52
Rosenberg, Isaac 51
Royal Army Medical Corps 52
Royal Flying Corps 30
Royal Naval Air Service 30
Russia 6, 7, 9, 24, 27, 38, 39

Sarajevo 8
Sassoon, Siegfried 14, 51
Schlieffen Plan 12
Serbia 9, 27
shell-shock 22
Sir Edward Grey 11
South Africa 24
Spanish flu 56, 57
Stevenson, Frances 38
suffragettes 61

tank 16, 35
Tonks, Henry 23
Treaty of London 10
trenches 13, 14, 15, 18, 20, 30, 31, 33
Triple Alliance 7
Triple Entente 7
Tsar Nicholas II 6
Turkey 9, 24, 27, 56
Turkish Empire 27

U-boats 29, 44
USA 29, 38, 56

Vice-Admiral Beatty 28
Vienna 11, 58
Voluntary Aid Detachment 52
von Moltke 12
von Richthoven, Baron 31

war bonds 41
war widows 4, 62
Western Front 13, 14, 15, 16, 18, 23, 31, 33, 34, 40
Westminster Abbey 63
Women's Auxiliary Army Corps 52, 63
Women's International League 55
Women's Peace Conference 55
Women's Peace Crusade 55
Women's Royal Air Force 53
Women's Royal Naval Service 53
Women's Land Army 39
Woodrow Wilson 57

Yeats, WB 30
Ypres 13, 15, 21, 32, 56, 57

zeppelin 46, 47, 60